Contents

Introduction

✳ • ✳

Welcome to a delicious learning experience—*Munch & Learn Math Story Mats*!

In these interactive math adventures, your students will use estimation to help the three little pigs build a house using pretzel sticks. They'll explore one-to-one correspondence as they help clowns add animal crackers to a circus train. They'll explore fractions as they count popcorn to eat at the movies. And much more! Here's how:

Math story mats are interactive math activities in which children listen to a story and use manipulatives to explore the math concepts presented in the story. Through the enticing lessons included in this book, children will learn important math concepts while organizing snack food on their mats. They'll place edible manipulatives such as raisins, crackers or popcorn on the appropriate place in the picture to "act out" the events in read-aloud math stories. In addition to the math mats, each lesson includes a page of appropriate reproducible manipulatives that can be used in place of edible ones.

Each story mat lesson is designed to meet your classroom needs and enhance the learning environment: Lessons are linked to one or more of the National Council of Teachers of Mathematics (NCTM) standards with an easy-to-read matrix of skills on page 6. Small cooperative groups, pairs, or individual children can use ready-to-go illustrated story mats. You'll also find easy-to-gather materials lists and management tips that make math learning a snap!

You'll whet children's appetite for math with these yummy, hands-on adventures. *Bon appetit*!

Why Edible Story Mats?

• ✳

✳ **Children need to experience math in the world around them.** When you involve the senses of touch, taste, and smell, children become eager and excited to explore math concepts. Story mats enhance the learning environment in ways that using paper and pencil alone simply cannot!

✳ **Children learn to follow verbal directions as well as to position items.** In doing so, their ability to follow directions will improve as they think through different strategies for solving math problems.

✳ **Child-friendly snacks come in a variety of shapes, colors, and sizes.** Such snacks make the perfect manipulatives for many math activities, adding interest and excitement.

✳ **After working with edible manipulatives at school, children might continue their learning experience at home.** At their own kitchen table, children can sort and count a packet of gummy snacks, count by groups using pretzel sticks, make patterns from different-shaped crackers, and more.

Important Story Mat Tips

Health and Safety

○ Before working with the edible manipulatives, have children wash their hands. You might also use antibacterial premoistened towelettes (found in many drugstores).

○ To make the distinction between snacking and the math activity clear, you might separate the food to be used on the story mat from the snack food. Munching and snacking can be done with food items that haven't been touched or handled previously during the math lesson. Or, have children eat their manipulatives for a snack after they've finished the lesson.

○ As always, when working with food, be aware of possible food allergies or restrictions. Ask parents or guardians to tell you of any concerns. The reproducible manipulatives included with each story mat may be used in place of edible manipulatives.

○ To keep the edible manipulatives fresh and ready to use, store them in self-closing plastic bags or airtight containers.

How to Use This Book

To enhance the lessons and build important math skills, the following features are included with each story mat:

◆ **Two Read-Aloud Stories** on one reproducible page. You can read these stories aloud for the initial lesson, and children can read them independently if they continue to work with the story mats.

◆ **A Target Skills List** lets you know the focus of each lesson.

◆ **Reproducible Manipulatives** for each story mat to use instead of edible manipulatives.

◆ **Steps** to follow as you use the story mat and its activities.

◆ **Math Talk:** questions and discussion ideas that help you encourage children to explain their reasoning and strategies.

◆ **Journal Extensions** offer ideas to help children extend their thinking with written or illustrated responses.

◆ **Assessment Tips** help you observe children's level of understanding.

◆ **Math Activities** extend the learning beyond the story mat.

Math story mats may be presented to children in a whole-group, small-group, or individual setting. You may give them to children to color, laminate them for future use, or copy each story mat onto heavy paper for repeated use. You can also simply make copies of the story mat for one-time use. If you use the reproducible manipulatives provided for each story mat, you might copy them onto heavyweight paper or laminate for added durability.

Meeting the NCTM Standards 2000

	Numbers and Operations	Estimation*	Number Sense and Numeration*	Concepts of Whole-Number Operations*	Whole-Number Computations*	Fractions and Decimals*	Patterns, Functions, and Algebra	Geometry and Spatial Sense	Measurement	Data Analysis, Statistics, and Probability	Problem Solving	Reasoning and Proof	Communication	Connections	Representation
Ants, Ants, Ants	●		●	●			●	●	●		●	●	●	●	●
A Day at the Circus	●		●	●	●		●	●			●	●	●	●	●
The Race	●		●	●			●	●		●	●	●	●	●	●
Ladybug Spots	●		●	●	●	●		●	●	●	●	●	●	●	●
The Store	●	●	●					●		●	●	●	●	●	●
Counting Sheep	●		●	●	●		●	●	●		●	●	●	●	●
The Fish Tank	●	●	●	●	●		●	●	●	●	●	●	●	●	●
The Movies	●	●	●	●	●	●		●			●	●	●	●	●
Sunflowers	●		●	●	●			●	●	●	●	●	●	●	●
The Circus Train	●		●	●	●			●	●		●	●	●	●	●
Farmers Market	●	●	●					●		●	●	●	●	●	●
Treasure Island	●	●	●	●	●			●	●		●	●	●	●	●
Tooth Tales	●		●	●	●		●	●	●		●	●	●	●	●
The Three Little Pigs	●	●	●			●		●			●	●	●	●	●
Dinosaur Dan	●	●	●				●	●			●	●	●	●	●

* Indicates a subcategory of Numbers and Operations

Ants, Ants, Ants

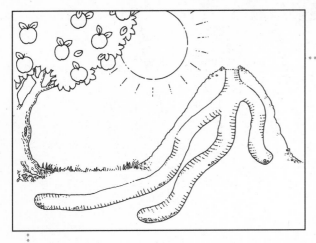

Read-Aloud Story 1: Antsy to Find a Home

Twenty ants were antsy to find a new home. They stood in a line near the apple tree. The line was so long that some of the ants had to stand on the side of a hill. One by one, they marched into the shortest tunnel. One, two, three, four. "We all won't fit. This tunnel will be too crowded," said the fifth ant. They all got out and lined up again.

"Let's go into the middle tunnel," said the first ant. They all tried to march in. One, two, three, four, five, six, seven, eight, nine, ten, eleven.

"We all won't fit. This tunnel will be too crowded," said the twelfth ant. They all got out and lined up again.

"Let's try the last tunnel," said one ant. They all tried to march in. One, two, three, four, five, six, seven, eight, nine, ten, eleven, twelve, thirteen, fourteen, fifteen, sixteen, seventeen, eighteen, nineteen, twenty!

"This is much more comfortable!" said the twentieth ant.

Read-Aloud Story 2: Happy Ants

On Monday, one happy ant played near the apple tree while one sleepy ant was asleep in the longest tunnel inside the anthill. On Tuesday, another happy ant came to play with the first happy ant near the apple tree. The same number of sleepy ants were asleep in the long tunnel inside the anthill. On Wednesday, another happy ant came to play with the two near the apple tree. The same number of sleepy ants were asleep in the long tunnel inside the anthill. On Thursday, another ant came, so all together four happy ants played tag near the apple tree. The same number of sleepy ants were asleep in the long tunnel inside the anthill. On Friday, another ant came, so all together five happy ants played near the apple tree. The same number of sleepy ants were asleep in the long tunnel inside the anthill. "Wake up! Wake up!" called the five happy ants. All of the sleepy ants in the tunnel woke up, crawled out of the tunnel, and went outside to play.

Antsy to Find a Home

Materials

* copies of Story Mat 1 (page 11)
* 20 raisins per child (or copies of manipulatives, page 12, 20 ants per child)

1 Distribute the story mats. Instruct children to just look at the mats and listen while you read through the story one time.

2 Distribute the raisins or paper manipulatives. Read through the story a second time, pausing after each sentence. As you do so, invite children to use the raisins or manipulatives to represent the ants in the story (markers may overlap). Check for understanding after each sentence.

Math Talk

* Did you estimate that the first tunnel would be too small?
* Did you estimate that the middle tunnel would be too small?
* Let's say half of the ants went into the medium-sized tunnel. Would they fit? Why or why not?

Journal Extension

Let children draw a picture of any number of ants marching in a straight line, and ask them to write a sentence describing the number of ants and where they are going. Or, invite them to write a story about being an ant. Would they rather take a nap in a tunnel or under a tree?

Here's More

Use the three construction paper strips from the assessment activity, (right). Next, distribute reproducible ant manipulatives (one sheet per child). Have children cut out the ants and lay them down on the three different strips. Ask children how many ants fit on each strip. Children can then present a number sentence: "My longest strip is [number of ants] long."

Read-Aloud Story 2

Happy Ants

Materials

✳ copies of Story Mat 1 (page 11)

✳ 10 raisins per child (or copies of manipulatives, page 12)

1 Distribute the mats. Instruct children to just listen and look while you read through the story one time.

2 Distribute the raisins or paper manipulatives and read through the story a second time, pausing after each sentence. Have children use the raisins or paper manipulatives to represent the ants in the story (markers may overlap). Check for understanding after each sentence.

Assessment TIPS

✦ From construction paper, children can cut three strips of paper of varying lengths. Ask each child to show you which strip is the longest, which is medium-sized, and which is shortest.

✦ Have a child retell the story (children might change the numbers and tunnels as they wish) as you or another child manipulates the ants. Notice if he or she uses ordinal numbers.

Target Skills

⚙ basic number facts (addition)
⚙ matching, one-to-one correspondence
⚙ comparison of numbers
⚙ order
⚙ position

Math Talk

✴ How many ants were playing together at the end of the story? (10) How can you check your work?

✴ What if the story continued, and more and more ants came to play tag and sleep in the tunnel? Can you continue telling the story, adding Saturday and Sunday?

Journal Extension

Let children work in pairs to use all of their raisins together on one story mat. Ask them to choose a number of ants to play near the apple tree and the same number of ants to be inside the tunnels. Have them write about the ants, describing how many are in each location and what they are doing.

Here's More

✴ Laminate copies of the read-aloud stories on page 7.

✴ Cut out a large rectangular shape from tan felt to use as a flannel board. Then use green, red, and brown felt to cut out shapes for an apple tree and anthill. Cut three strips of tan felt for tunnels and ten small black circles for ants.

✴ Place the felt pieces in a self-sealing plastic bag. Prepare a notebook that includes a parent page encouraging families to share the "flannel board" and the read-aloud stories and to create new stories of their own. On the blank pages, each family can write down a simple story.

✴ Place the notebook, the laminated story pages, and the felt pieces in an inexpensive backpack or tote bag that zips shut for children to take home. After each family returns the kit, share the stories they wrote.

Assessment TIPS

◆ Were children able to place the same number of ants inside the tunnels as were outside near the apple tree? To evaluate their understanding of one-to-one correspondence, point to groups of different numbers of objects in the room. Ask children to place the same number of manipulatives in a group on their desks.

◆ Ask children to think of other objects they can use to count to ten (fingers, toes, items found in the classroom, and so on). Have children count them aloud for you.

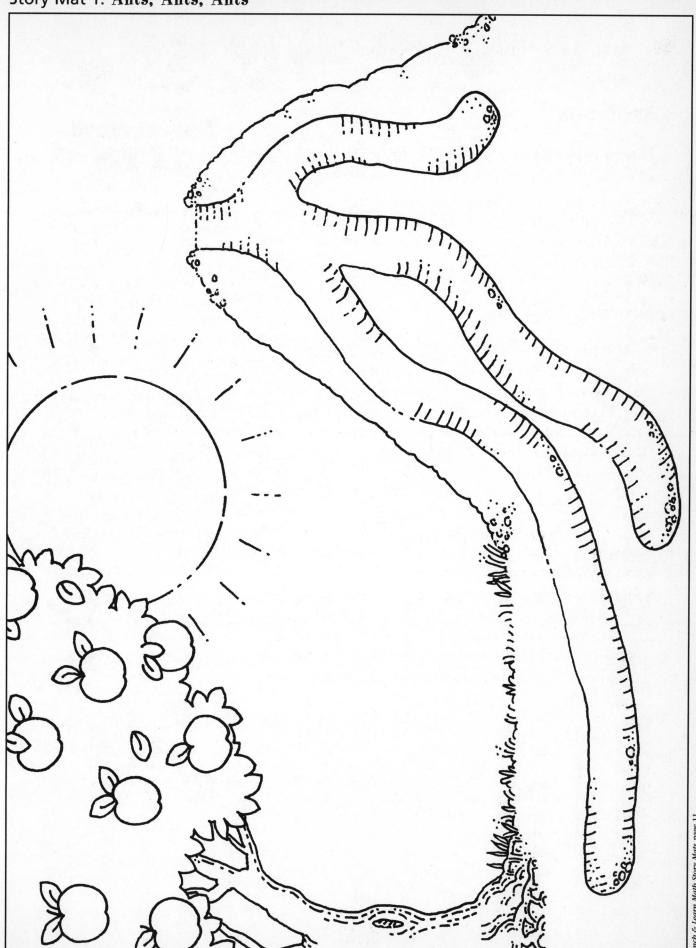

Munch & Learn Math Story Mats, page 11
Scholastic Professional Books

Story Mat 1: Ants, Ants, Ants: Manipulatives

A Day at the Circus

Read-Aloud Story 1: On With the Show!

The circus is about to begin! Hurry, hurry, step right up! One seal balances one ball on its nose. Two dogs ride two unicycles down a ramp. Three clowns each hold a balloon. Four bears each balance on a ball like ballerinas.

Isn't the circus fun? Now sit back and enjoy the show!

Read-Aloud Story 2: Who Goes First?

The ringmaster announces every circus act in the show. Who goes first? The act with the most performers goes first. Will it be the dogs, the bears, the seal, or the clowns?

The ringmaster shouts, "The four bears will go first!" Give them each a ball to use for their tricks.

Who goes second? The circus act with one less performer than the bears. The ringmaster shouts, "The three clowns will go second!" Give them each a balloon to hold. Who goes third? The circus act with one less performer than the clowns.

The ringmaster shouts, "The two dogs will go third!" Give them each a wheel. Who goes fourth? The circus act with one less than the dogs.

The ringmaster shouts, "The one seal will go fourth!" Give the seal one ball. Now clap for the circus show! Hip, hip, hooray!

On With the Show

Materials

✳ copies of Story Mat 2 (page 17)

✳ 10 small round crackers per child (or copies of
manipulatives, page 18; 5 balls, 3 balloons, and
2 wheels per child.)

Target Skills

❂ one-to-one correspondence
❂ counting
❂ basic number facts (addition)

1 Distribute the mats. Instruct children to just listen and look while
you read through the story one time.

2 Distribute the crackers or paper manipulatives and read through
the story a second time, pausing after each sentence. Have children
use the crackers or paper manipulatives to represent the wheels,
balls, or balloons in the story. Check for understanding after
each sentence.

Math Talk

✳ Do you see a pattern in the story? Tell about it.

✳ How many animals are there all together in the circus at the end of
the story?

✳ How many balls, balloons, and wheels are there all together at the
end of the story?

✳ What if there were five elephants balancing balls on their trunks at
the circus? How many crackers would you add to the picture? How
many crackers would there be all together at the circus?

Journal Extension

Have children draw other animals performing with balls at the circus.
Instruct them to draw one ball for each animal and write a sentence
describing the circus act.

Make multiple copies of the story mat so that if you cut out just the bears, each student will have ten bears (for instance, if you have 20 students, copy the story mat 50 times, cut out the bears, and distribute ten bears to each child). Photocopy ten balls for each child from the manipulatives on page 18 and distribute. (Store in self-sealing plastic bags for future use.) Have children use the bears and balls to answer word problems such as:

✳ If four bears did tricks at the circus, how many balls would they use? What if one of those bears left with his ball? How many bears and balls would remain?

✳ If six bears did tricks, how many more bears would need to join the act to make ten all together?

✳ Five bears balanced on balls for the circus show. If two bears left, but forgot to take their balls with them, how many bears and balls were left?

Assessment TIPS

◆ To see if children understand the concept of one for each, divide the class into small groups of various sizes. Ask each group to tell you how many crackers that group should get if each person gets one. Count aloud together as you distribute crackers to each group for a snack. Older children might try counting by twos and getting two crackers each.

Read-Aloud Story 2

Who Goes First?

Materials

✳ copies of Story Mat 2 (page 17)

✳ 10 small round crackers per child (or copies of manipulatives, page 18; 5 balls, 3 balloons, and 2 wheels per child).

Target Skills

◎ order of events
◎ comparing numbers
◎ basic number facts (subtraction)
◎ one-to-one correspondence

1 Distribute the mats. Instruct children to just listen and look while you read through the story one time.

2 Distribute the crackers or paper manipulatives and read through the story a second time, pausing after each sentence. Have children use the crackers or paper

manipulatives to represent the wheels, balls, or balloons in the story. Check for understanding after each sentence.

Math Talk

✳ How would the order of events have changed if the ringmaster wanted the circus act with the fewest performers to go first? Have children retell the story and describe which acts would come next by using the words *one more than*.

✳ Do you see a pattern in the story? Tell about it.

Journal Extension

Children can write sentences or draw a series of pictures to describe the order of events for an activity (baking cookies, getting dressed, taking the dog for a walk, and so on). Encourage them to use the ordinal numbers *first*, *second*, *third*, and *fourth* in their sentences or to label their pictures.

Here's More

Divide the class into four groups. Using craft sticks, paper plates, tape, and crayons or markers, each group can make stick puppets of bears, clowns, dogs, and seals, one kind per group. (Attach craft sticks to paper plates with masking tape.) Read through the story several times, letting children take turns acting out the story in front of the group with their puppets. You might also vary the numbers each time.

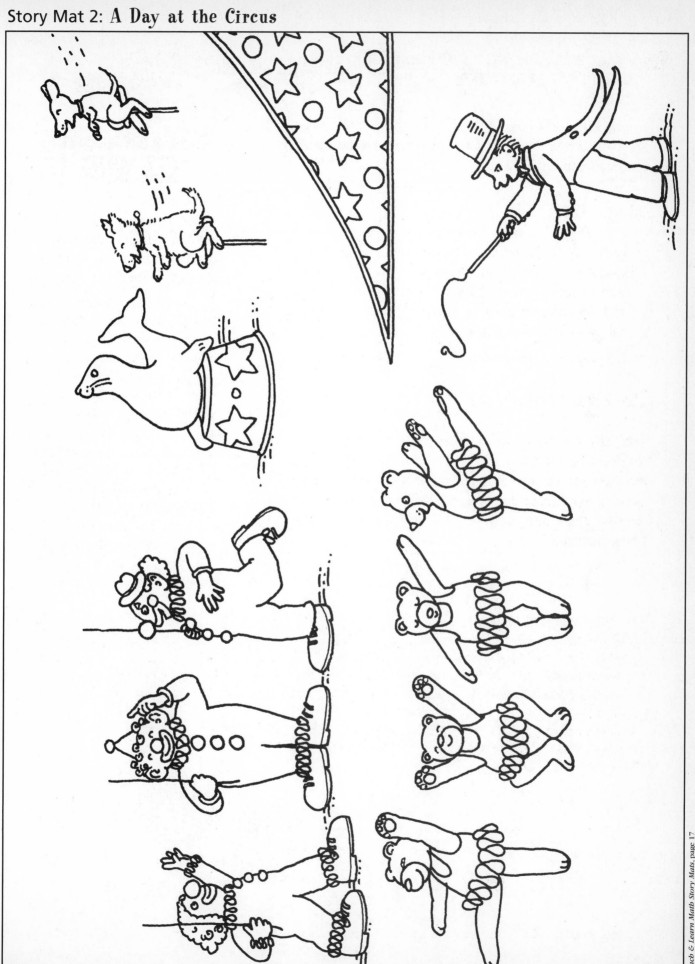

Story Mat 2: A Day at the Circus: Manipulatives

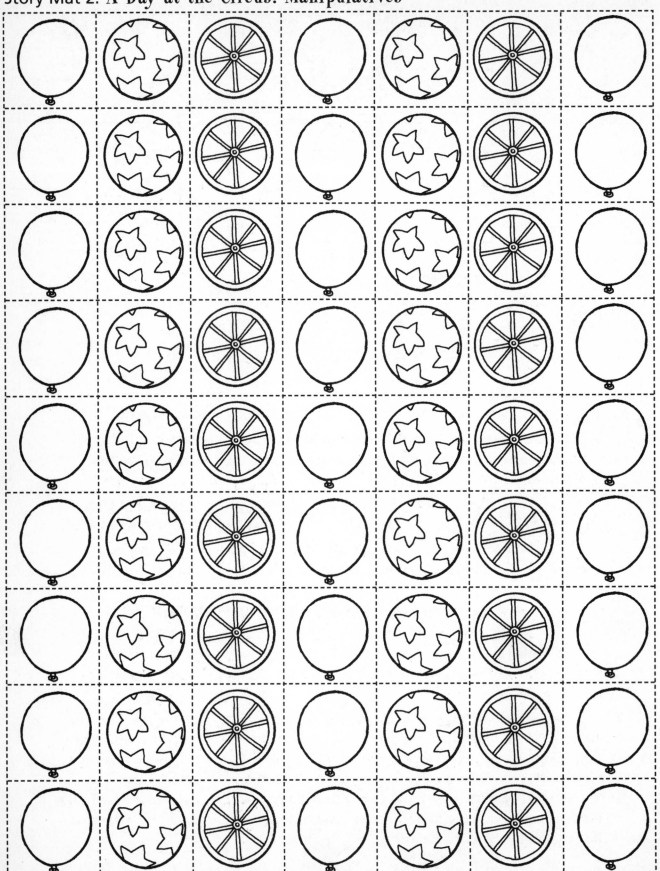

The Race

Read-Aloud Story 1: The Finish Line

The flags are waving! The race is over! Put two matching shapes on the flags. These shapes have four sides of equal length. What are they called?

Race car Number Five reached the finish line first! Hooray, hooray! Put two matching shapes on the cones at the finish line. These shapes have three sides. What are they called?

The race cars have stopped. Their wheels have stopped turning. Put four matching shapes on all the wheels. These shapes are round. What are they called?

What other shapes do you see on the racetrack? Put matching shapes on every shape you find. It's been an exciting day!

Read-Aloud Story 2: Who Will Win?

It's time for the race to start again. But first, each car needs two round wheels. The man needs two square flags. Great! Now they're ready to start. On your mark, get set, go!

Vroom! Vroom! Two race cars speed around and around the track. The cars speed past the signs along the track. Put a round marker on the first round sign. Put square markers on the next two signs. Put a triangle marker on the next sign. Now put a round marker on the next sign. What pattern do you see? Use your markers to finish the pattern along the line of signs. *Vroom! Vroom!* The race cars are heading toward the finish line. Put two triangles on the finish line. Which car do you think will win the race?

The Finish Line

Materials

✳ copies of Story Mat 3 (page 23)

✳ small square, round, and triangular crackers,
10 of each shape per child (or copies of
manipulatives, page 24)

Target Skills

✿ counting
✿ shape identification
✿ matching

1 Distribute the mats. Instruct children to just listen and look
while you read through the story one time.

2 Distribute the crackers or paper manipulatives and read
through the story a second time, pausing after each sentence.
Have children use the crackers or paper manipulatives to
represent the shapes in the story. Check for understanding
after each sentence.

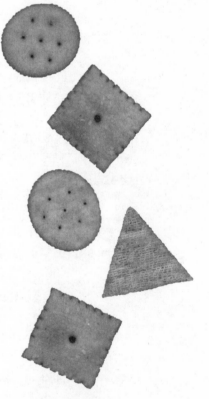

Math Talk

✳ Can you name the shapes you found on the story mat? What
else is shaped like a triangle, square, or circle?

✳ Count how many of each shape you found. How could we
make a bar graph to show how many of each shape there are?
(To do this, make a bar graph with three columns, one for each
shape. Arrange the manipulatives, by shape, in the columns on
the graph, to represent their numbers on the story mat.)

Journal Extension

Ask children to draw and label their own circles, squares, and
triangles in different sizes and colors.

Have children each cut three pieces of construction paper into a large square, circle, and triangle, writing their name on each. They pick up one of their paper shapes and stand next to an object in the classroom that matches the shape. When everyone is standing next to an object, ask volunteers to name the paper shapes and the matching items. When finished, build a bar graph with the paper shapes on the floor (separate the three columns with jump ropes or yard sticks). Count and compare the results.

Assessment TIPS

◆ Have children point out objects shaped like circles, squares, and triangles in the classroom.

Read-Aloud Story 2

Who Will Win?

Materials

* copies of Story Mat 3 (page 23)

* small round, triangular, and square crackers, 8 of each shape per child (or copies of manipulatives, page 24, at least 10 of each shape per child)

Target Skills

◉ shapes
◉ counting
◉ position
◉ order
◉ patterns
◉ one-to-one correspondence

1 Distribute the mats. Instruct children to just listen and look while you read through the story one time.

2 Distribute the crackers or paper manipulatives and read through the story a second time, pausing after each sentence. Have children use the crackers or paper manipulatives to represent the shapes in the story. Check for understanding after each sentence.

Math Talk

✳ Can you use your markers to make a new pattern on the back of your story mats? Describe the pattern you used.

✳ How did you identify the pattern in the story? What would it look like if it continued?

Journal Extension

Invite children to draw three new patterns. For the first pattern, use shapes. For the second, use letters (such as AABAAB). For the third, use numbers (such as 123123). (Younger children can draw all three patterns using shapes.)

Here's More

Give children strips of paper and have them draw a pattern across the first half of the strip. Help them pair off and switch strips with their partners. Each child will finish drawing the other's pattern. Partners can then share the patterns with the class.

Story Mat 3: The Race

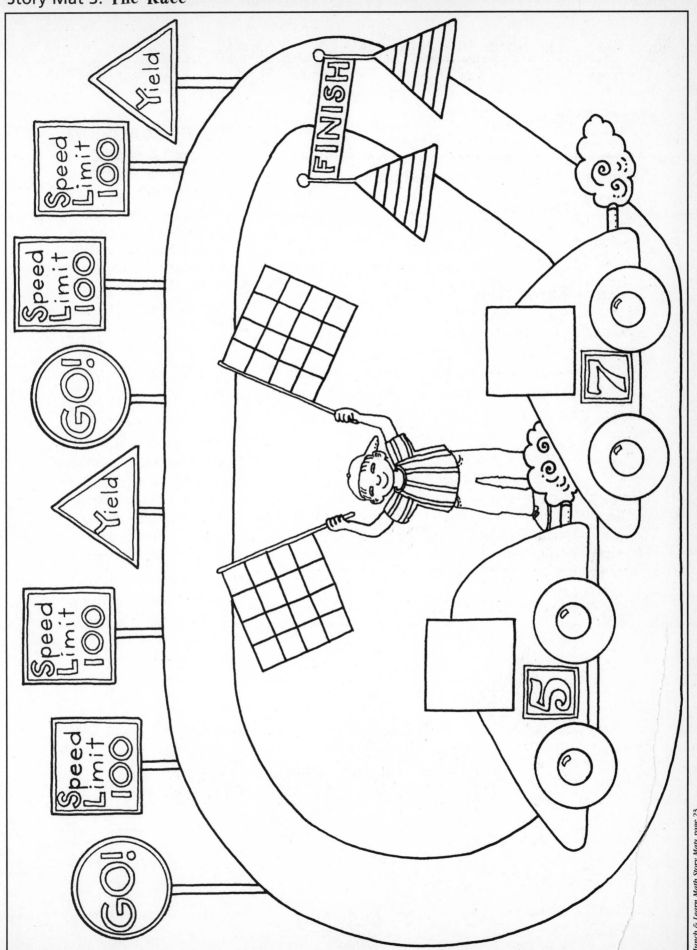

Story Mat 3: The Race: Manipulatives

Ladybug Spots

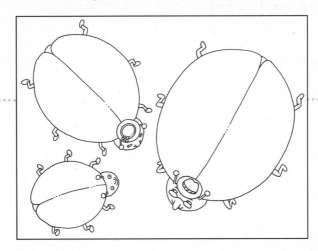

Read-Aloud Story 1: Happy Birthday, Butterfly!

Today is Butterfly's birthday, and she's having a birthday party! She and her friends are playing a special game called "Put the Spots on the Bug." First it is Butterfly's turn! She puts two spots on the smallest ladybug so that each wing has the same number of spots. Then she puts four spots on the medium-sized ladybug so that each wing has the same number of spots. Finally, Butterfly puts six spots on the biggest ladybug so that each wing has the same number of spots.

What a fun game! Happy birthday, Butterfly!

Read-Aloud Story 2: Bath Time for Ladybugs

Scrub-a-dub-dub! It's bath time for the ladybug family. Little Ladybug has two spots on her wings. Mama Ladybug has four spots. And Papa Ladybug has six spots!

Take your bath, Little Ladybug. First count your spots. Scrub-a-dub-dub. Scrub away one spot. How many spots are left? Scrub the rest away. Now you're nice and clean! Take your bath, Mama Ladybug. First count your spots. Scrub-a-dub-dub. Scrub away two spots. How many spots are left? Scrub these away, one by one, until you're nice and clean! Now take your bath, Papa Ladybug. Count your spots. Scrub-a-dub-dub. Scrub away 3 spots. How many spots are left? Scrub these away, one by one, until you're nice and clean! Now bath time is over for the ladybug family. Scrub-a-dub-dub!

Happy Birthday, Butterfly!

Materials

* copies of Story Mat 4 (page 29)
* 12 raisins per child (or copies of manipulatives, page 30, 12 spots per child)

1 Distribute the mats. Instruct children to just listen and look while you read through the story one time.

2 Distribute the raisins or paper manipulatives and read through the story a second time, pausing after each sentence. Have children use the raisins or paper manipulatives to represent the spots in the story. Check for understanding after each sentence.

Math Talk

* Can you explain how you divided the spots equally between the wings of each ladybug so that each wing had the same number of spots?

* Can you put the spots on the wings of the ladybugs so that the patterns of spots on both wings are symmetrical, or the same on both sides? Can you think of other things that are symmetrical?

Journal Extension

Have children draw a picture of a ladybug or write about a time they saw one. If they have never seen a ladybug before, ask them to draw a picture or write about a ladybug they'd like to see or to have as a pet. How many spots would it have?

·:·Here's More·:·

Have children create a delicious and edible ladybug while further exploring symmetry. Each child needs a vanilla wafer, red frosting, black pastry frosting, and mini chocolate chips. Children spread the red frosting on top of the wafers and use the black pastry frosting to make a head and a line down the middle. Children can design their own ladybugs using the mini chocolate chips to create symmetrical wings.

Assessment TIPS

✦ Encourage children to show you how they would divide different amounts of manipulatives into two equal parts (use an even number of manipulatives to avoid confusion).

Read-Aloud Story 2

Bath Time for Ladybugs

Materials

✳ copies of Story Mat 4 (page 29)

✳ 1 small box of raisins per child (or copies of manipulatives, page 30, 18 spots per child)

Target Skills

✪ counting
✪ comparing numbers
✪ basic number facts (addition, subtraction)

1 Distribute the mats. Instruct children to just listen and look while you read through the story one time.

2 Distribute the raisins or paper manipulatives and read through the story a second time, pausing after each sentence. Have children use the raisins or paper manipulatives to represent the spots in the story. Check for understanding after each sentence.

Math Talk

✳ How many spots did you give to each ladybug?
Which ladybug had the most spots? Which ladybug
had the fewest? Did any of the ladybugs have the
same number of spots?

✳ How many spots did the ladybug family wash away
all together? How do you know?

✳ Make number sentences that explain what you did
on each ladybug.

Journal Extension

Have children use their journals to create and write
word problems with different ladybugs, comparing and
adding their spots. Children can illustrate pictures to
accompany their word problems.

Here's More

Draw a large ladybug on the board and ask a volunteer
to draw spots on the ladybug's wings. Count the spots in
unison and write that number on the board. Explain that
it's bath time for the ladybug, and time to scrub away its
spots. As children take turns coming to the board to erase
different spots, help them write number sentences on the
board to show their work.

Assessment TIPS

◆ To see if children
understand the concept
of comparing numbers,
ask them to put a differ-
ent number of raisins or
spots in three different
piles. Have them count
each pile and record the
number in each. Children
can tell which pile had
the most, second most,
and fewest spots.

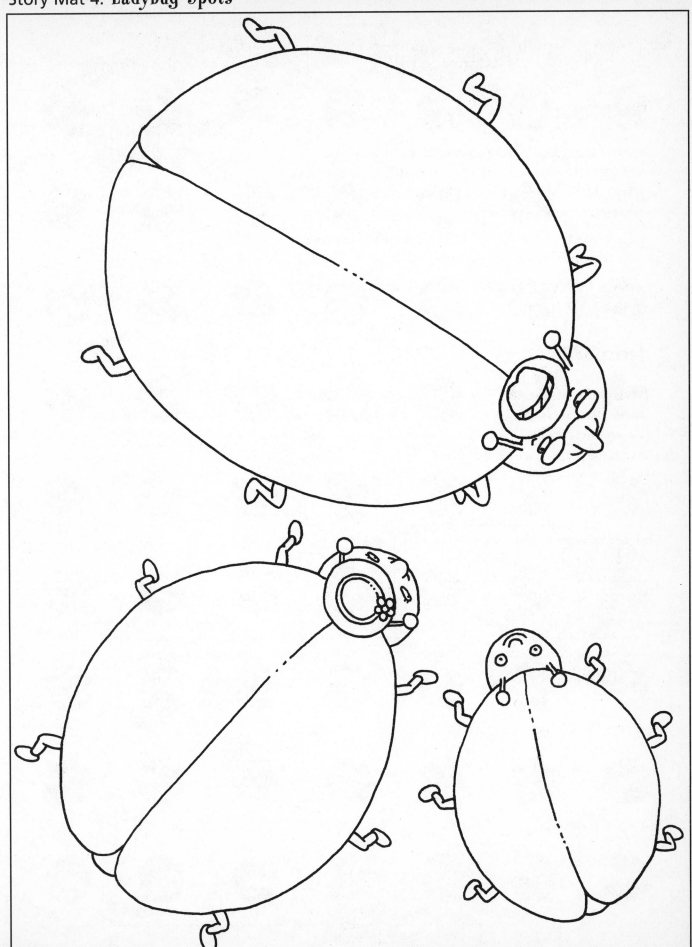

Story Mat 4: Ladybug Spots: Manipulatives

The Store

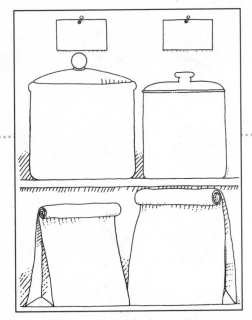

Read-Aloud Story 1:
The Candy Store

You own a candy store! Yummy! It's time for you to fill the jars of candy. The sign on the big jar needs an even number on it: 2, 4, 6, or 8. Put that number of candy pieces inside the big jar.

The sign on the small jar needs on odd number on it: 1, 3, 5, 7, or 9. Put that number of candy piececs inside the small jar.

Mrs. Lopez walks into your candy store. "My son, Carlos, is turning eight," she says. "We're having a piñata filled with candy. Since eight is an even number, I want to buy an even number of candies to put in the piñata." Should Mrs. Lopez buy the candy in the small or big jar? Count the candy she buys and put it in either one of the bags.

Read-Aloud Story 2: The Button Store

The button store is having a button sale! Choose two different numbers. Put the larger number on the sign for the big jar. Put the smaller number on the sign for the small jar. Now use your markers to put the number of buttons in each jar that it says on each sign.

Look! Here come two cowboys. "We need buttons to put on our shirts," the cowboys say. The tall cowboy says, "I need more buttons than my partner because my shirt is bigger." The short cowboy says, "I need fewer buttons than my partner because my shirt is smaller." Which jar of buttons does the tall cowboy buy? Count those buttons and put them in the big bag. Which jar of buttons does the short cowboy buy? Count those buttons and put them in the small bag. *Yippee-yi-yay!* Ride 'em cowboy!

The Candy Store

Materials

* copies of Story Mat 5 (page 35)

* numeral-shaped cookies (available in large grocery stores), several even and several odd per child (or copies of manipulatives, page 36)

* small candy pieces in a paper cup, at least 18 per child (or copies of manipulatives, page 36)

1 Distribute the mats. Instruct children to just listen and look while you read through the story one time.

2 Distribute the cookies and candy or paper manipulatives and read through the story a second time, pausing after each sentence. Have children use the cookies and candy or paper manipulatives to represent the signs and candy in the story. Check for understanding after each sentence.

3 Read through the story several more times. Each time, choose a volunteer's name to put in the story in place of Carlos and change the age to match the volunteer's age. Ask children to determine whether the age is an even or an odd number and change the story ending accordingly.

Math Talk

* Is your own age an even or an odd number? Use manipulatives to show your reasoning.

* Can you count by 2's? Is 2 an even number or odd number? How do you know?

Journal Extension

Ask children to draw the outline of a piñata and then draw an even or odd number of candies inside. Have them record the number next to the piñata, along with the word *even* or *odd*.

Fill a jar with candy and let children guess the number of pieces inside. Record all guesses and determine whether each guess is an even or an odd number. Then pour out the candy and have children organize the pieces into a line of pairs to see if there is one left over or not. Practice skip-counting as you count the pieces in unison to determine the total.

Read-Aloud Story 2

The Button Store

Materials

* copies of Story Mat 5 (page 35)

* numeral-shaped cookies (available in large grocery stores), several different numbers per child (or copies of manipulatives, page 36)

* small candy pieces in a paper cup, at least 18 per child (or copies of manipulatives, page 36)

Target Skills

◎ size
◎ basic number facts (addition)
◎ counting
◎ comparison

1 Distribute the mats. Instruct children to just listen and look while you read through the story one time.

33

2 Distribute the cookies and candy or paper manipulatives and read through the story a second time, pausing after each sentence. Have children use the cookies and candy or paper manipulatives to represent the signs and buttons in the story. (Students should choose amounts of less than 12, so that manipulatives are manageable.) Check for understanding after each sentence.

Math Talk

✳ What if there had been a third cowboy, a medium-sized one? Try retelling the story to include him.

✳ Does anyone in the class have a shirt with buttons on it? How many kids have shirts with buttons on them? Try comparing the number of buttons on different shirts. Does anyone have more buttons on his or her shirt than another shirt? Fewer? The same amount?

Journal Extension

Have children work with partners to make a two-column chart in their journals, labeling one column "More" and the other "Less." Then ask them to draw pictures of the number of markers they placed in the big jar and the number of markers they placed in the small jar under the correct heading. The chart should also include pictures to show their partner's markers.

Assessment TIPS

◆ Children might act out the story. Provide cowboy hats, button-down flannel shirts of different sizes, and bandanas. Choose two volunteers of different heights to play the parts. For props, use markers or buttons and two clear jars of different sizes. Before each play is performed, have the class choose a large number and a small number. They can then fill the two jars with that number of markers or buttons, making a sign for each. The cowboys can buy the corresponding jars of buttons. Use the provided dialogue, or have children make up new lines.

Here's More

As children become comfortable comparing piles of markers that number fewer than ten, have them use handfuls of markers to learn to compare two piles of larger numbers. First have them estimate the number of markers they think are in each pile and record their guesses. Have them circle the larger number. Then ask them to count the number of markers in each pile and record the actual answer. Ask children to tell you how their guesses compared with the actual answers.

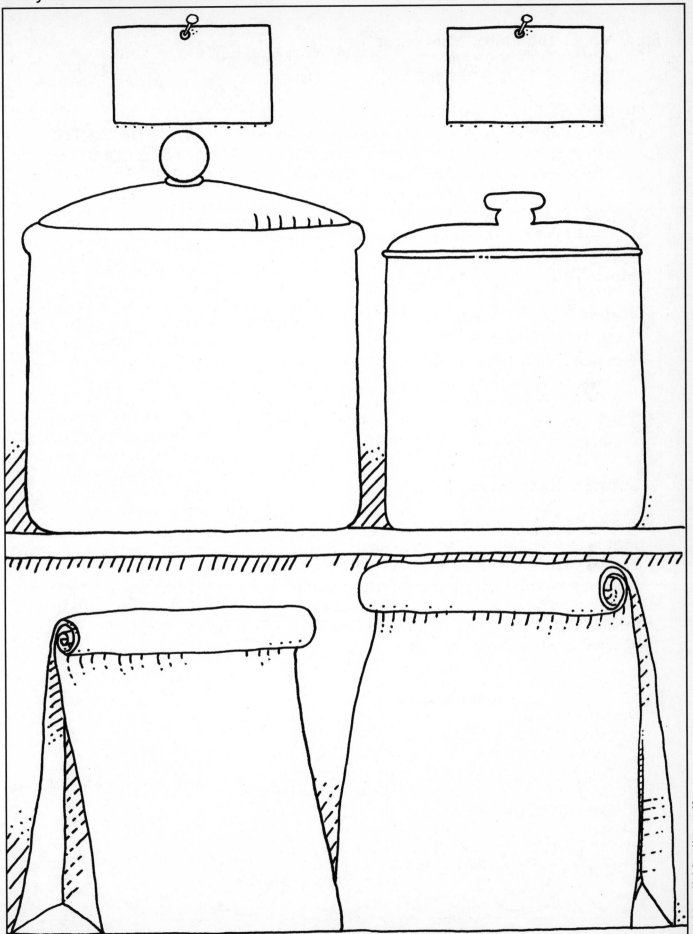

Story Mat 5: The Store: Manipulatives

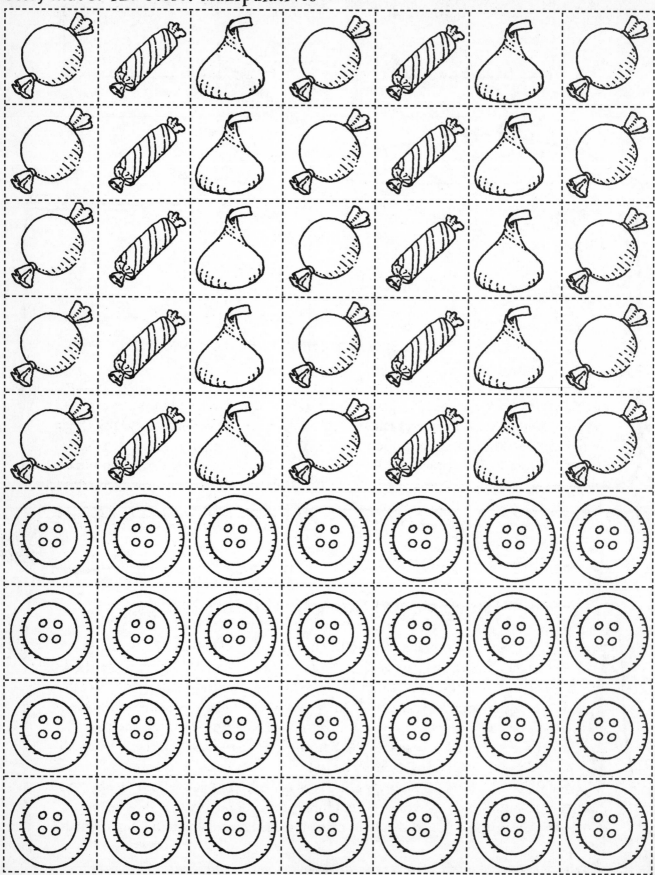

Counting Sheep

Read-Aloud Story 1: Go to Sleep, Suzie!

Sleepy Suzie can't fall asleep! First, she tries counting the sheep in her picture of Little Bo-Peep. Put a piece of popcorn on each sheep she counts: one, two, three, four, five. Sleepy Suzie still can't fall asleep! Second, she tries counting the toy sheep on her shelves. Put a piece of popcorn on each sheep she counts: 1, 2, 3, 4, 5, 6, 7. Sleepy Suzie still can't fall asleep! Third, she tries counting the ten sheep she hopes to see in her dreams. 1, 2, 3, 4, 5, 6, 7, 8, 9, 10. Put a piece of popcorn for each of the sheep in her dream balloon. Sleepy Suzie starts to feel sleepy. In her dreams, she counts the ten sheep by twos. 2, 4, 6, 8, 10. Sleepy Suzie is almost asleep. Then, in her dreams, she counts the ten sheep by fives. 5, 10. Z-z-z-z-z.

Good night, Sleepy Suzie! Sleep tight!

Read-Aloud Story 2: Making Ten

Sleepy Suzie likes to make ten. On her bed are six teddy bears. How many teddy bears should Sleepy Suzie add to her bed to make ten? Add them to her bed. In the picture of Little Bo-Peep, there are five sheep. How many sheep does Sleepy Suzie add to the picture to make ten? On the toy shelves, there are four teddy bears on the bottom shelf. Sleepy Suzie puts three teddy bears on top of the shelves. She puts three more teddy bears on the bottom shelf. Are there ten teddy bears all together on the toy shelves? Count them and see!

Yawn! It's time for bed. Sleepy Suzie closes her eyes and falls asleep. Sleepy Suzie even likes to make ten in her dreams! Put three sheep in her dreams. How many sheep does Sleepy Suzie need to add to make ten? Add those sheep too. Nighty, night!

Go to Sleep, Suzie!

Materials

* ✳ copies of Story Mat 6 (page 41)
* ✳ cup of popcorn, about 30 pieces per child
  (or copies of manipulatives, page 42)

1 Distribute the mats. Instruct children to just listen and look while you read through the story one time.

2 Distribute the popcorn or paper manipulatives and read through the story a second time, pausing after each sentence. Have children use the popcorn or paper manipulatives to represent the sheep in the story. It's fine if some of the markers overlap. Check for understanding after each sentence. (It's fine if some of the markers overlap.)

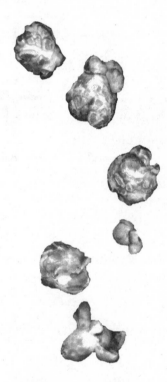

Math Talk

* ✳ Which is faster: counting by ones or skip-counting?
* ✳ Which is the fastest way to count to ten: by ones, by twos, or by fives? How do you know?

Journal Extension

After children practice skip-counting, have them draw a row of ten pieces of popcorn or sheep grouped in pairs. Help them label their drawings 2, 4, 6, 8, and 10 beneath the groupings. Repeat the activity with two groupings of five pieces of popcorn.

Have children race to fill bags with popcorn and practice counting at the same time. Give each child 20 pieces of popcorn and a small bag. Have one child place the popcorn in the bag, counting by ones. Have another child do the same, counting by twos. Have a third child do the same, counting by fives. Who fills the bag first, second, and last?

Assessment TIPS

◆ Have children count popcorn to show you the different ways they know how to skip-count. Ask which way of counting was easier or faster.

◆ Distribute bite-sized bear-shaped crackers or gummy candy, or the reproducible manipulative bears. Change the story to have Sleepy Suzie count all the bears in her room as she falls asleep. Notice if children are comfortable with skip-counting.

Read-Aloud Story 2

Making Ten
Materials

* copies of Story Mat 6 (page 41)

* bear-shaped graham crackers or gummy bears, 10 per child (or copies of manipulatives, page 42)

* cup of popcorn, at least 15 pieces per child (or copies of manipulatives, page 42)

Target Skills

◉ counting
◉ sums to ten
◉ basic number facts (addition)
◉ position

1 Distribute the mats. Instruct children to just listen and look while you read through the story one time.

2 Distribute the popcorn or paper manipulatives and read through the story a second time, pausing after each sentence. Have children use the edible or paper manipulatives to represent the sheep and bears in the story. (It's fine if some of the markers overlap.) Check for understanding after each sentence.

Math Talk

✳ How did you know how many markers Sleepy Suzie needed to make ten in each situation? Can you think of another way you might have arrived at your answer?

✳ How many bears were in Suzie's room when she fell asleep? How many sheep?

Journal Extension

Have children choose one addition example from the story to record in their journal. Instruct them to first draw a picture of the equation and then to write a corresponding number sentence. Or, have them write a story about counting things before they fall asleep and a corresponding number sentence.

Here's More

Help children make 10's frames from posterboard with ten 2-inch squares. Children can use their popcorn or manipulatives on their frames to solve word problems, such as:

✳ If Sleepy Suzie has 5 sheep, how many sheep does she need to add to make 10?

✳ If Sleepy Suzie bought 4 teddy bears to give as birthday presents, how many more teddy bears would she need to buy to make 10?

Sleepy Suzie's Dreams

《Little Bo Peep》

Story Mat 6: Counting Sheep: Manipulatives

The Fish Tank

Read-Aloud Story 1:
A Day at the Aquarium

The class was on a field trip to the aquarium. The children looked into a big tank. Inside they saw many different kinds of fish. Use your fish to show what they saw. Todd saw two yellow fish swimming near a cave. Anna saw five striped fish swimming by the big green plant. Carrie saw four blue fish resting by a big rock. How many fish did they see all together?

The friends took a closer look.

"Look!" shouted Todd. "There are more fish at the top of the tank!" He pointed to two more fish.

"Look!" said Anna. "I see more fish too!" Anna pointed to three fish swimming near the diver.

"I see one more!" cried Carrie. She pointed to the cave. One fish swam out. How many fish did the friends see all together?

Read-Aloud Story 2: How Many Fish?

The children were looking into the tank when they saw a scuba diver swim by. The scuba diver was measuring the things that were in the tank.

But what was the diver doing? He wasn't measuring with a ruler. He was measuring with—fish!

"I wonder how high that plant is?" said Todd. Write down your guess. Then stack your fish head to tail, to measure the height of the plant.

"I wonder how wide the rock is?" said Anna. Write down your guess. Then place your fish side by side, head to tail, to measure the length of the rock.

Just then the fish the diver was using to measure with swam away. Carrie reached into her backpack and pulled out a ruler.

"Maybe he would like to measure with this instead!"

A Day at the Aquarium

Materials

٭ copies of Story Mat 7 (page 47)

٭ fish-shaped crackers, gummy fish, or Swedish fish, 12 per child (or copies of manipulatives, page 48)

1 Distribute the mats. Instruct children to just listen and look while you read through the story one time.

2 Distribute the edible or paper manipulatives and read through the story a second time, pausing after each sentence. Have children use the edible or paper manipulatives to represent the fish in the story. (It's fine if some of the markers overlap.) Check for understanding after each sentence.

Math Talk

٭ Where did you place the fish on your mat?

٭ How many more fish did children see the second time they looked into the tank?

Journal Extension

Have children draw a fish tank in their books. Let them choose what they will place in the aquarium (rocks, plants, and so on) and use the manipulatives to create math story problems of their own. Have them write or dictate one of the problems in their journal.

✳ Help children pair off. Using fish as markers, one child puts down a handful of fish. Their partner counts the fish and records the number. Then, while the partner closes her eyes, the first player puts down more fish. The second player must then figure out how many fish were added and record the new total. Players then switch roles and play again.

✳ Children can play the game in reverse! The first player puts down a larger number of fish and records the number. Then, while the second player closes his eyes, the first player removes some of the fish. The second player figures out how many were removed.

Assessment TIPS

◆ See if children can add together the fish in the picture. Try giving them different combinations, such as "Add the fish by the cave to the fish at the bottom of the tank."

Read-Aloud Story 2

How Many Fish?
Materials

✳ copies of Story Mat 7 (page 47)

✳ a cup of fish-shaped crackers or gummy or Swedish fish, about 12 per child (or copies of manipulatives, page 48)

✳ paper and pencil

Target Skills

◌ size
◌ estimating
◌ nonstandard measurement (length, width, height)

1 Distribute the mats. Instruct children to just listen and look while you read through the story one time.

2 Distribute the edible or paper manipulatives and read through the story a second time, pausing after each sentence. Have children use their edible or paper manipulatives to measure each item. Check for understanding after each sentence.

Math Talk
. . . . *

* If you had used a ruler, would everyone's answer have been the same? (Discuss the difference between standard and nonstandard measurement.)

* Which measurement was the longest? Shortest?

* Were your estimates close to the actual measurement?

Journal Extension
. . . . *

Have children draw an item of their choice in their journals. Then have them use the fish to measure the length of that object and record their results. Older children might also use a ruler.

Here's More

Give each child a paper fish manipulative sheet to take home and cut apart. Ask children to measure objects in their home using the manipulatives and record their results. Have them bring their lists back to class and describe what they measured.

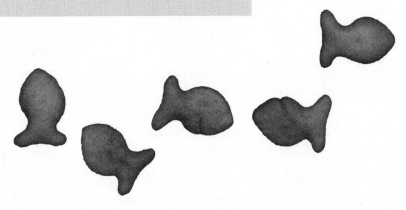

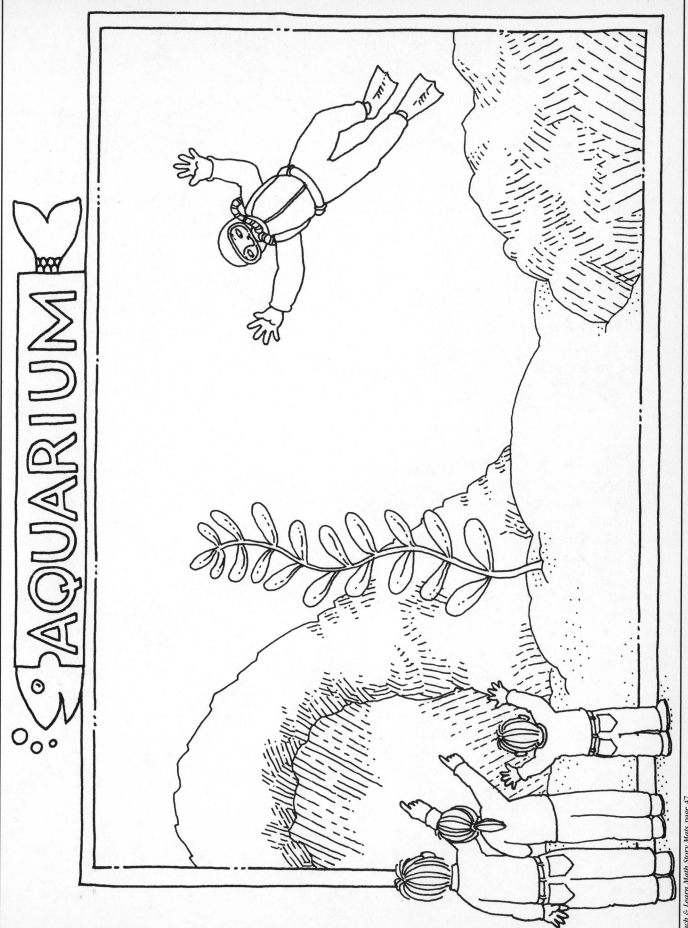

Story Mat 7: The Tank: Manipulatives

The Movies

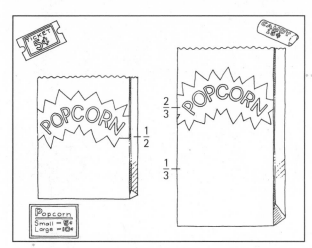

(Children will need a working knowledge of money amounts up to 25 cents to complete the activity.)

Read-Aloud Story 1: Popcorn!

"Let's go to the movies," Ben said.

"Great!" said Sara. "Let's buy popcorn, too!"

At the movies, they stood in line for popcorn. "I just want a small popcorn," Sara said.

Sara watched as they filled her bag of popcorn. First they filled it one-half full. Use pieces of popcorn to fill Sara's bag to the line that says one-half. How many more pieces of popcorn do you think are needed to fill the bag to the top? Count out that much popcorn and add it to the bag. Did you guess too many, too few, or just the right amount?

"I want a large popcorn," Ben said. First they filled it one-third full. Use pieces of popcorn to fill Ben's bag to the line that says one-third. Next, they filled it two-thirds full. Continue using pieces of popcorn to fill Ben's bag to the line that says two-thirds. Last, they filled it to the top. Use pieces of popcorn to fill Ben's bag to the top of the bag. "Yum!" Ben said. "Now it's time for the movie!"

Read-Aloud Story 2: Going to the Movies

Timmy and Tammy, the twins, went to see a movie. They each had a quarter to spend. Put two quarters on the edge of your mat. Put your handful of change next to the mat.

First Timmy bought a ticket with his quarter. Trade the quarter for the same amount in change and place the correct coin amount on the ticket. How much money does Timmy have left? Then Timmy spent all the rest of his money on something to eat. What do you think he bought? Put the correct amount of coins on it to show what you think he chose. Then remove all the coins from the mat.

Tammy bought her ticket, too. Trade the quarter for the same amount in change and place the correct coin on the ticket. Then she decided to buy candy. Place the money on the candy. How much change does Tammy get?

Tammy planned on buying more movie tickets tomorrow with her leftover change. How many tickets will she be able to buy?

Popcorn

Materials

✳ copies of Story Mat 8 (page 53)

✳ about 2 cups of popped popcorn per child (or copies of popcorn manipulatives, page 54, 30 pieces of popcorn per child)

1 Distribute the mats. Instruct children to just listen and look while you read through the story one time.

2 Distribute the popcorn or paper manipulatives and read through the story a second time, pausing after each sentence. Have children use the popcorn or paper manipulatives to fill the bag as described. Check for understanding after each sentence.

Math Talk

✳ How many pieces of popcorn did you use to fill Sara's bag to the $\frac{1}{2}$ line? Why do you think that some of you have different answers? (Guide students to notice that pieces of popcorn are not the same exact size.)

✳ Can you think of anything else that can be divided into thirds? (pizza, pie, cake)

✳ How close was your estimate when you filled Ben's bag to the $\frac{1}{3}$ line? Did your estimates get closer when you filled the bag to the $\frac{2}{3}$ line and then to the top? Why? (Guide students to notice that estimates are more accurate when based on prior knowledge.)

Target Skills

◎ size
◎ fractions
◎ estimating
◎ counting
◎ basic number facts (addition)
◎ nonstandard measurement (volume)
◎ order

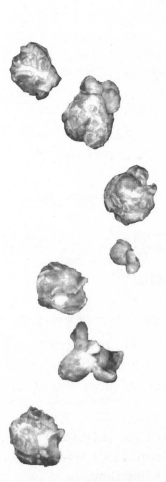

Journal Extension

Have children illustrate or write about a time they went to the movies and bought popcorn. Did they buy a small, medium, or large popcorn? How much of it did they eat? Or, they can write a story about what it would be like to be a kernel of popcorn.

Here's More

Reinforce subtraction skills with word problems such as:

* Ben had a full bag of popcorn. He ate one-third of the popcorn. How full was the bag now?

* Sara's popcorn bag was half full. She ate two pieces of popcorn. How many pieces of popcorn were in the bag now?

* Sara had a full bag of popcorn. She ate six pieces when the movie started. She ate three more pieces in the middle of the movie. At the end of the movie, how many pieces did she eat if she ate all the rest?

Read-Aloud Story 2

Going to the Movies

Materials

* copies of Story Mat 8 (page 53)

* coins or copies of coin manipulatives, page 54: at least two quarters, four dimes, six nickels, and twenty pennies for each student

1 Distribute the mats. Instruct children to just listen and look while you read through the story one time.

Target Skills

* size
* fractions
* estimating
* counting
* basic number facts (addition)
* nonstandard measurement (volume)
* order

2 Distribute the coins or paper manipulatives and read through the story a second time, pausing after each sentence. Have children use the coins or paper manipulatives to work out each problem. Check for understanding after each sentence.

Math Talk

✳ How did you figure out the change each twin received? Can you describe your reasoning?

✳ Is there more than one way of solving the problems? (Guide students to notice that Timmy, for example, may have bought a combination of a small popcorn and candy or two large popcorns.)

Journal Extension

Have children draw and list different combinations of items the twins could have bought at the movies with their quarters if they didn't have to buy any tickets.

Here's More

Provide toy catalogs for children to browse through. Have each child cut out pictures of toys and glue them to a piece of construction paper, or draw toys of their choice. Instruct them to draw price tags on each toy. Give each child a business-size envelope (a "wallet") to hold coins or reproducible manipulatives. Partners can play a game in which one pretends to purchase items from the second student's pictures, pay for them, and receive change. Then have children switch roles.

Assessment TIPS

◆ Are children able to determine the correct amount of change for different purchases? Set up a "store" with several items marked with price tags and pretend to purchase various items. Have children pretend to be the store owner and give you change.

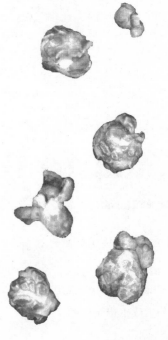

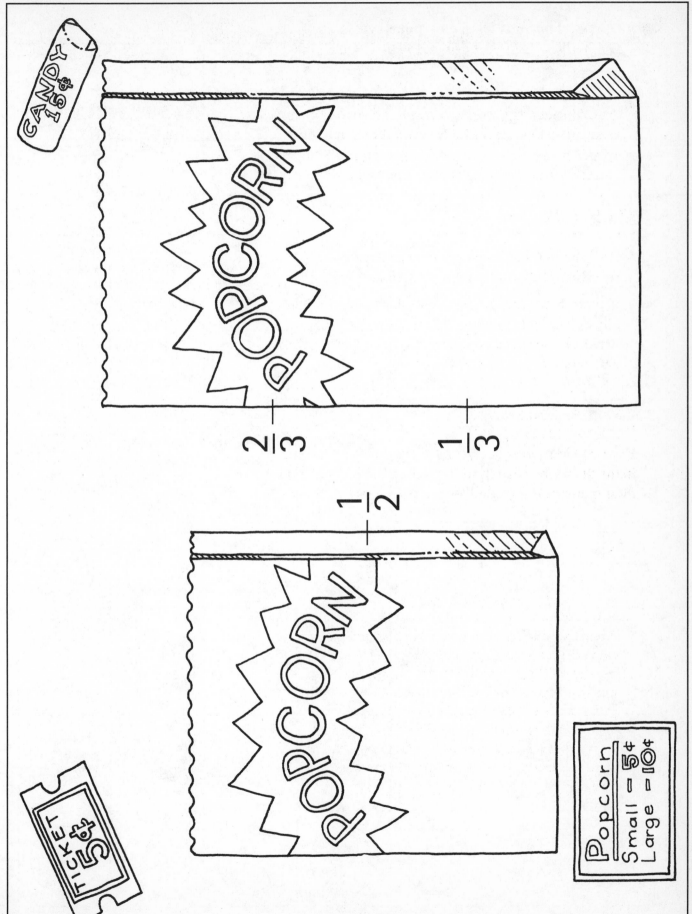

Story Mat 8: The Movies: Manipulatives

Sunflowers

Read-Aloud Story 1: Sunflower Seed Pie

Six sunflowers stood in the garden. Each sunflower held seven seeds.

Chris Crow and Mario Crow flew down and landed in the garden. "Let's make a sunflower seed pie," Chris Crow said. He picked three seeds from each sunflower and put them in a pile. How many did he pick in all?

"I LOVE sunflower seed pie!" Mario Crow cawed. He picked two more from each sunflower and put them in a new pile. How many did he pick in all?

Chris Crow and Mario Crow brought all the seeds to their kitchen and made a big, delicious sunflower seed pie. How many seeds did they use in all?

Now look at the sunflowers. Count the seeds that are left in each. Do you think there are enough for the crows to make another pie the same size as their last one? Yum, yum!

Read-Aloud Story 2: Seeds for the Sunflowers

Chris Crow and Mario Crow had twelve sunflower seeds. "Look!" said Chris Crow. "These sunflowers don't have any seeds. Let's give them ours."

"Great idea!" Mario Crow cawed. "Let's give the three sunflowers in the top row each a group of four seeds." He took twelve seeds and made equal groups of four seeds on three of the sunflowers.

"Wait!" said Chris Crow. "Some of the sunflowers still don't have any seeds. Put the seeds all back in a pile and try again."

This time Mario Crow took twelve seeds and made equal groups of three seeds on four of the sunflowers. "How's this?" he asked.

"Better," Chris Crow said. "But some of the sunflowers still don't have any seeds. Put the seeds all back in a pile and try again."

This time Mario Crow gave all six sunflowers an equal number of seeds. Divide up twelve seeds on the sunflowers to show what he did.

Sunflower Seed Pie

Materials

❋ copies of Story Mat 9 (page 59)

❋ paper cups of shelled or unshelled sunflower seeds, at least 45 per child (or copies of manipulatives, page 60)

1 Distribute the mats. Instruct children to just listen and look while you read through the story one time.

2 Distribute the sunflower seeds or paper manipulatives and read through the story a second time, pausing after each sentence. Have children use the sunflower seeds or paper manipulatives to represent the seeds in the story. (The paper seeds can overlap.) Check for understanding after each sentence.

Target Skills

☸ counting

☸ basic number facts (addition, subtraction, multiplication, division)

☸ comparing numbers

Math Talk

❋ Write a number sentence to show how many seeds Chris Crow took compared to how many seeds Mario Crow took.

❋ How did you figure out how many seeds each crow picked in all? (Encourage children to describe the different strategies they used.)

❋ At the end of the story, how could you tell if there were enough seeds for the crows to make another pie the same size as the last? How can you prove that?

Journal Extension

Have children draw a few sunflowers in their journal, draw seeds in the center of each flower, count the seeds in each and record the numbers. Ask them to write or dictate a sentence describing which sunflower has more seeds than the other does. Encourage them to use the words *greater than* and *less than* in their writing.

Provide opportunities for children to practice comparing numbers with Sunflower Math. Here's how:

* Have children make two sunflowers with yellow construction paper and craft sticks. Have them write a different number on each sunflower's center and draw the corresponding number of seeds.

* Have children compare the two numbers and determine which has more seeds and which has less seeds.

* Fill two paper cups with dried beans for weight. Label one cup "More" and the other cup "Less." Invite children to come forward and "plant" their sunflowers in the appropriate cups.

Assessment TIPS

◆ Ask each child to show you a different combination of numbers to get enough seeds to make a sunflower seed pie.

◆ Do students understand the concept of most and least? Ask them to compare the number in different groups of objects in the room and tell you which group has the most and which group has the least.

Read-Aloud Story 2

Seeds for the Sunflowers

Materials

* copies of Story Mat 9 (page 59)
* 12 sunflower seeds per child (or copies of manipulatives, page 60)

Target Skills

◎ counting
◎ basic number facts (addition, subtraction, multiplication, division)
◎ grouping

1 Distribute the mats. Instruct children to just listen and look while you read through the story one time.

2 Distribute the seeds or paper manipulatives and read through the story a second time, pausing after each sentence. Have children use the seeds or paper manipulatives to represent the seeds in the story. (It's fine if some of the markers overlap.) Check for understanding after each sentence.

Assessment TIPS

Ask children to divide different numbers of sunflower seeds into equal groups and have them explain their reasoning.

Math Talk

✳ Why do you think the crows had a hard time dividing up the seeds at first?

✳ What strategy do you use when you want to share equally? (for example, one for each child, then two for each child, and so on)

Journal Extension

Ask children to illustrate or write about how they would make a sunflower seed pie! How many seeds will they need? How many sunflowers will they gather the seeds from, and in what groupings? What are the ingredients in their pie? How do they cook it?

Here's More

Divide the class into small groups and give each group four paper plates and a bowl of sunflower seeds. Have children work in groups to follow your directions for word problems, such as:

✳ Take three plates and nine seeds. Divide the seeds evenly into three groups.

✳ Take two plates and eight seeds. Divide the seeds evenly into two groups.

✳ Take four plates and four seeds. Divide the seeds evenly into four groups.

Story Mat 9: **Sunflowers**

Munch & Learn Math Story Mats, page 59
Scholastic Professional Books

Story Mat 9: **Sunflowers: Manipulatives**

The Circus Train

Read-Aloud Story 1: Helping the Clowns

The animals got loose from the cars on the circus train! Can you help the clowns put them back on the train? Put one furry animal in the front car that is just behind the engine. Put one horned animal in the middle car. Put one climbing animal in the last car. Each car should have a different animal in it.

Now more animals have to find the right cars to ride in! Can you help the clowns? Find all the animals that match the one in the first car and add them to that car. Now find all the animals that match the one in the middle car and put them all in the middle car. Now find all the animals that match the one in the last car and put them all in the last car. Now how many animals are in each car?

Three cheers for the circus! Hip, hip, hooray!

Read-Aloud Story 2: The Circus Parade

There were three circus animals in the front car of the train, right behind the engine. There were three animals in the middle car. There were four animals in the last car.

One clown said, "Let's play a game and make a parade! We'll roll a number cube. The number we get will be the number of animals we take off the train to put in our circus parade."

The clowns rolled a four. They took two animals from the front car. How many animals should they take from the last car? Take them and use your markers to start a parade line across the bottom of the mat. Then the clowns rolled a one. Take an animal from the middle car to add to the parade.

What number do the clowns need to roll in order to get the rest of the animals in line? Try rolling your number cube to get that number. Roll your number cube until all of the animals are in the parade.

Hurrah, hurrah! Sis, boom, bah! Here comes the parade!

Helping the Clowns

Materials

✳ copies of Story Mat 10 (page 65)

✳ various animal-shaped cookies, crackers, or gummy candy (each child should have at least two matching of each shape and at least three different kinds of animals), about 12 per child (or copies of manipulatives, page 66)

1 Distribute the mats. Instruct children to just listen and look while you read through the story one time.

2 Distribute the edible or paper manipulatives and read through the story a second time, pausing after each sentence. Have children use the edibles or paper manipulatives to represent the animals in the story. Check for understanding after each sentence.

Math Talk

✳ Can you describe the differences in the animals you have? Try to use adjectives such as *furry*, *horned*, *climbing*, and so on.

✳ Can you think of another way to organize the animals in the circus train?

✳ Could some animals go in more than one group? (For example, the monkey could go in both the furry and the climbing group.)

Target Skills

☼ classifying
☼ counting
☼ position
☼ order
☼ one-to-one correspondence
☼ sorting
☼ matching

Journal Extension

Have children draw their own circus train and explain how they decided to group the animals in it.

Here's More

Have children choose two or three animals to compare and contrast using a Venn diagram.

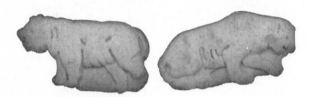

Read-Aloud Story 2

The Circus Parade

Materials

* copies of Story Mat 10 (page 65)

* various animal-shaped cookies, crackers, or gummy candy, 10 per child (or copies of manipulatives, page 66)

* number cubes, one per child

Target Skills

- counting
- order
- position
- basic number facts (addition, subtraction)

1 Distribute the mats. Instruct children to just listen and look while you read through the story one time.

2 Distribute the edible or paper manipulatives and read through the story a second time, pausing after each sentence. Have children use the edible or paper manipulatives to represent the animals in the story and a number cube to act out the clowns' actions. Check for understanding after each sentence.

Math Talk

✳ Imagine that the clowns could only roll the number cube twice. What numbers would they need to roll to get all of the animals off the train? How do you know?

✳ Make some number sentences that describe things that happened in the story.

Journal Extension

Have children draw a circus train with animals in it and write a sentence that describes how many animals are in it and what would happen if two got off, three got off, and so on. Help children write number sentences that match their sentences.

Here's More

Have children perform this story as a play. Choose volunteers to be the clowns and the animals. Place sheets or fabric on the floor in a line to represent the circus cars. The animals can sit on the fabric when they are in the cars. Change the story to keep rolling the number cube until all the animals are in the parade. After the clowns make the parade, let them lead the animals in a march around the room, playing lively music as they go.

Assessment TIPS

◆ Ask children to describe different combinations of animals the clowns could have chosen for each roll of the number cube. (For example, for a roll of four, the clowns could have taken three from the first car and one from the last car.)

◆ Ask children to explain their addition or subtraction strategies as they moved the manipulatives on their mats.

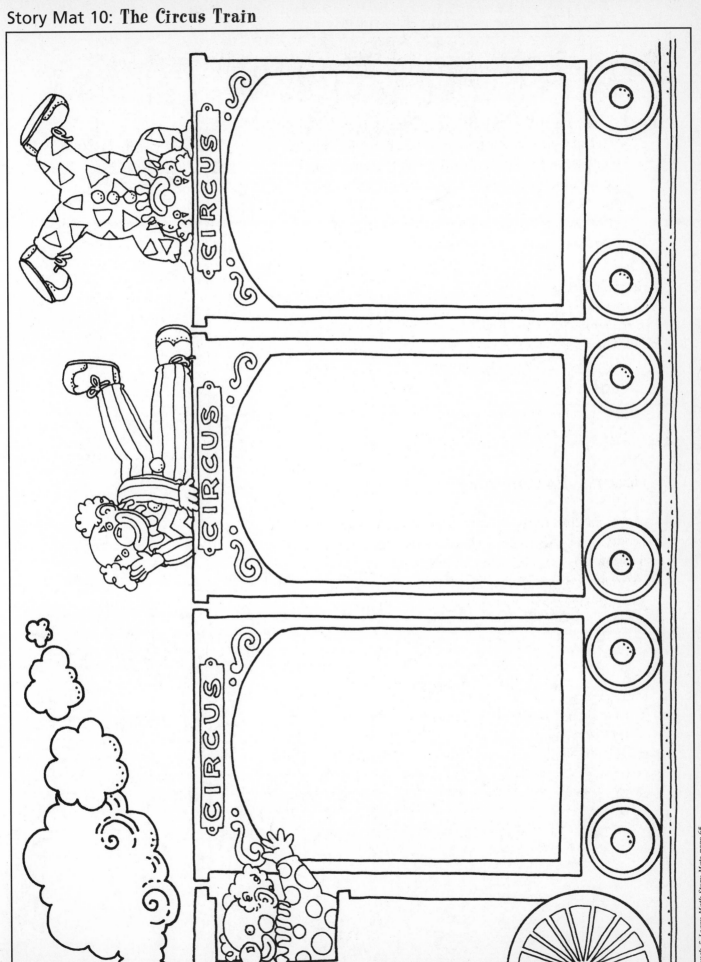

Story Mat 10: The Circus Train: Manipulatives

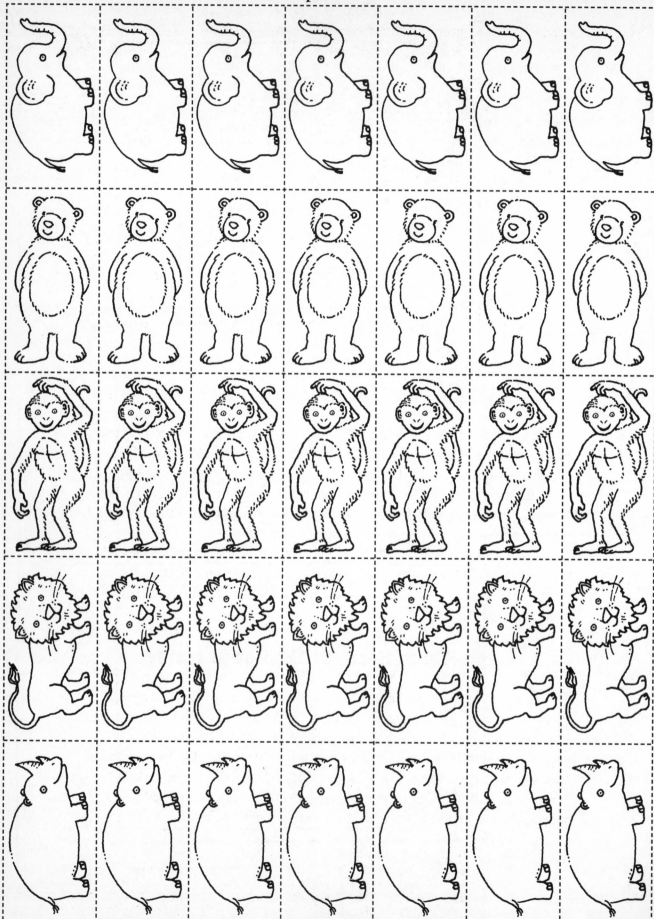

Farmers Market

Read-Aloud Story 1: Harvest Time

It's fall! Farmer Brown's family is up early helping with the harvest. Farmer Brown is in the fields. He picks 12 ears of corn. Mr. Brown's daughter is in the orchard. She picks 10 ripe apples. Mr. Brown's son is in the garden. He picks 8 bright orange carrots. "Lunchtime!" calls Mrs. Brown. Everyone drops his or her harvest in a big pile and runs toward the house. Put the food in a pile next to your mat.

After lunch, the Browns come out of the house with full bellies and three baskets. The Browns need to put all the apples in one basket, the carrots in the second basket and the corn in the third. Can you help them sort the harvest?

Read-Aloud Story 2: Market Surprise

Farmer Brown's market is open for business. There are 12 apples, 8 carrots, and 6 ears of corn in the baskets. Mr. Stevens is his first customer. Silly Mr. Stevens loves to play games. Today he decides to play a game while he shops. "I want to buy 10 things today. I am going to close my eyes and pick out a total of 10 things from these baskets." Mr. Stevens pulls out 10 things and stops. Which item do you think he will pull out most often? Which item will he have the least of? Try it yourself to find out.

Harvest Time

Materials

* copies of Story Mat 11 (page 71)

* cup of apple-flavored cereal or handful of cinnamon candies per child (or one copy of manipulative page per child, page 72)

* cup of mini carrot sticks per child (or one copy of manipulative page per child, page 72)

* cup of candy corn per child (or one copy of manipulative page per child, page 72)

Target Skills

⊙ making comparisons
⊙ sorting

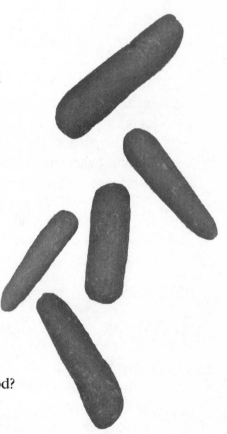

1 Distribute the mats. Instruct children to just listen and look while you read through the story one time.

2 Distribute the edible or paper manipulatives. Read through the story a second time, pausing after each sentence. Have children use the edible or paper manipulatives to represent the harvest items in the story. (It's fine if some of the markers overlap.) Check for understanding after each sentence.

Math Talk

* How many of each item are in each basket?

* Which basket has the most food?

* Which basket has the least food?

* Are there any other ways you could have sorted the food?

Journal Extension

Put a bowl of fruit or vegetables in front of the class. As a class, count how many of each item is in the bowl. Invite

students to compare the fruits or vegetables by writing or drawing a number sentence (for example, 10 pieces of fruit – 6 pears = 4) that shows how many more of one item there is compared to another.

Here's More

Use a Venn diagram to practice comparing and contrasting. Instead of comparing "apples to oranges" your students will compare two foods grown on a farm—an apple and a tomato.

✳ First, display one red apple next to one red tomato.

✳ Ask students to make observations about the two items

✳ Next, make a Venn Diagram (two overlapping hula hoops, two circle-shaped pieces of yarn, or two overlapping circles on the board).

✳ Label the rings with index cards marked "Tomato," "Apple," and "Both."

✳ Discuss with students what the two items have in common. These ideas go in the overlapping section of the circles. What is unique to the tomato? This goes in the tomato part of the diagram. What is unique to the apple? This goes in the apple part of the diagram.

✳ Remember—apples and tomatoes are both fruits!

Assessment TIPS

◆ Place a colorful variety of socks in a laundry basket. Watch as each child sorts the socks into matching pairs. Ask: Are there any other ways to sort the socks other than into pairs? How might you sort them? By color? By size?

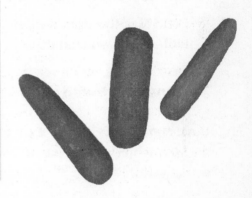

Read-Aloud Story 2

Market Surprise

Materials

✳ copies of Story Mat 11 (page 71)

✳ apple-flavored cereal or cinnamon candies, 12 pieces per child

✳ mini carrot sticks, 8 per child

✳ candy corn, 6 pieces per child

Target Skills

☺ probability
☺ counting

1 Distribute the mats. Instruct children to just listen and look while you read through the story one time.

2 Distribute the edible or paper manipulatives and read through the story a second time, pausing after each sentence. Have children use the edible or paper manipulatives to represent the harvest items in the story. (It's fine if some of the markers overlap.) Check for understanding after each sentence.

Math Talk

* Will the results be the same each time the game is played?

* Were your results the same as someone else's results?

* Could Mr. Stevens end up choosing ten of a single item? If yes, which one?

Journal Extension

Have children write about or illustrate the item they guessed would fill the basket first, and which one actually did.

Here's More

Invite children to play the game again. Have them keep a tally of how many times they picked an apple, corn, or carrot to make ten items. When finished, make a class graph of each student's tally marks for use in comparing the results.

Story Mat 11: **Farmers Market: Manipulatives**

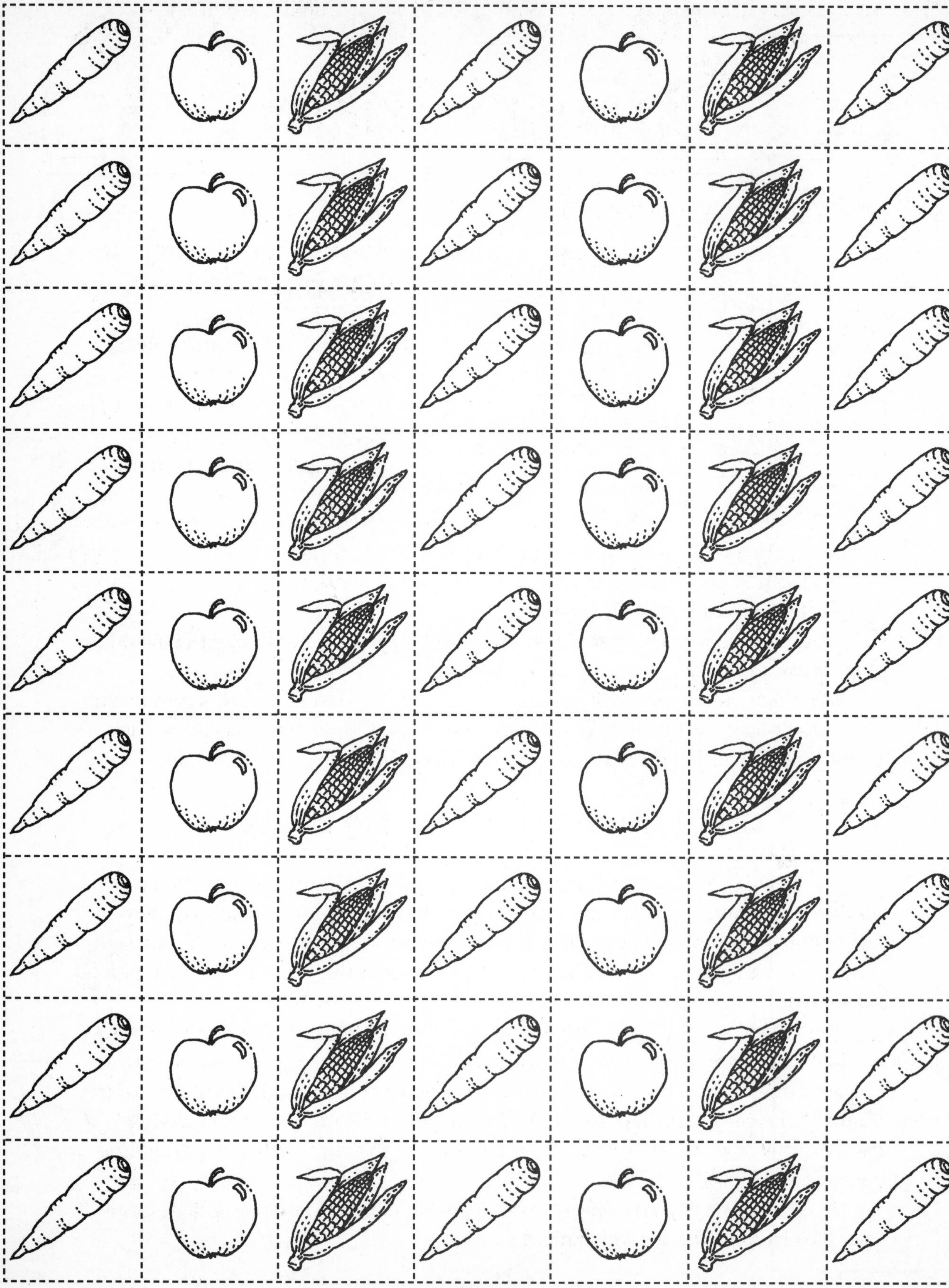

Munch & Learn Math Story Mats, page 72
Scholastic Professional Books

Treasure Island

Read-Aloud Story 1: Digging for Gold

Michael and his sister Heather were walking on the beach. Suddenly they saw something sticking out of the sand.

"It's a giant treasure chest!" cried Michael.

Michael and Heather opened the lid and looked inside. They counted 20 gold coins inside.

"What will we do with all of the coins?" asked Heather.

"Let's figure it out," said Michael.

"A new train set will cost eight coins," said Michael. He took eight coins out. How many are left?

"The new bike I want will cost six coins," said Heather. She took six coins out.

"Don't forget Mom and Dad's anniversary! The picture frame will cost five coins," said Michael. Will the kids have enough gold coins to buy this gift?

Read-Aloud Story 2: Buried Treasure

On Monday, Michael and Heather found three gold coins buried in the sand on Treasure Island. They put the coins in their treasure chest. On Tuesday, they found four more coins! They added them to their treasure chest. On Wednesday, they found three more coins. They added the coins to the chest. How many did they have?

On Thursday, there was a big storm. Heather and Michael's treasure chest was washed out to sea. They found the treasure chest later that afternoon but four coins were missing. They decided to look for more coins on a different part of the island. When they went looking on Friday they found more gold coins hidden in a dark, dark cave, so there were enough coins to fill the chest until it was full! Use your markers to fill the chest.

Now it's Saturday and they're counting their coins! How many gold coins do they have? Count the markers and see.

Digging for Gold

Materials

* copies of Story Mat 12 (page 76)

* cup of round cereal per child (or copies of manipulatives, page 77)

* paper and pencil

1 Distribute the mats. Instruct children to just listen and look while you read through the story one time.

2 Distribute the cereal or paper manipulatives and read through the story a second time, pausing after each sentence. Have children use the cereal or paper manipulatives to represent the gold coins in the story. (It's fine if some of the markers overlap.) Check for understanding after each sentence.

Math Talk

* How did you figure out if the kids had enough gold coins to buy the anniversary gift?

* What if the anniversary gift cost seven gold coins?

Journal Extension

Have children draw their own treasure chest in their journal. Then have them draw coins to fill the chest and estimate how many are in the chest. After they count the coins, children can record the actual amount.

Target Skills

☺ basic number operations (subtraction)
☺ counting
☺ comparison

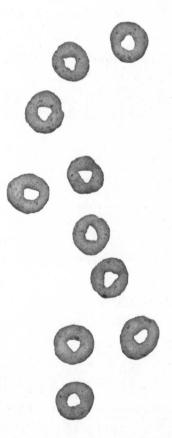

Make a subtraction center using a small box (made to look like a treasure chest) and yellow game chips. Place a box of index cards with treasure-themed word problems next to the box. For instance, A Pirate has put 14 pieces of gold in his treasure chest. Polly, his parrot, thinks the coins are food and takes 6. How many are left?) Children draw a card and use the manipulatives to solve the problem.

Assessment TIPS

◆ Tell children to cross out a certain number of coins in their treasure chests. Invite children to write the number sentence they made. For example: If there are 16 coins in a child's treasure chest and you say the number 7, the child puts an "X" on 7 coins and writes the number sentence 16 – 7=9.

Read-Aloud Story 2

Buried Treasure

Materials

* copies of Story Mat 12 (page 76)

* cup of circle-shaped cereal per child (or copies of manipulatives, page 77)

* paper and pencil

Target Skills

◯ order
◯ counting
◯ basic number facts (addition, subtraction)
◯ measurement (volume)

1 Distribute the mats. Instruct children to just listen and look while you read through the story one time.

2 Distribute the cereal or paper manipulatives and read through the story a second time, pausing after each sentence. Have children use the cereal or paper manipulatives to represent the gold coins in the story. (It's fine if some of the markers overlap.) Check for understanding after each sentence.

Math Talk
. . . . ✳

✳ How many coins were left in the treasure chest after the storm hit? Can you write this as a number sentence?

✳ How might you guess how many coins would fill the chest? (Answers may vary depending on the type of manipulative used.)

Journal Extension
. . . . ✳

Help children make a chart with the days of the week in their journals. Have them choose a number of manipulatives to put under each day. Children can add up how many coins they have by the end of the week.

Here's More

Divide the class into small groups. Have each small group rewrite the story to use different numbers of gold coins. Have the groups write number sentences for each day of the week that show what happened in the new story. Let each group share its new story with the rest of the class. Have the listeners work out the new stories on their story mats. (More manipulatives may be needed for each child to accommodate the changes.)

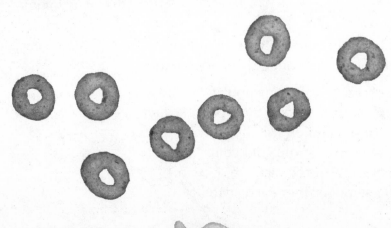

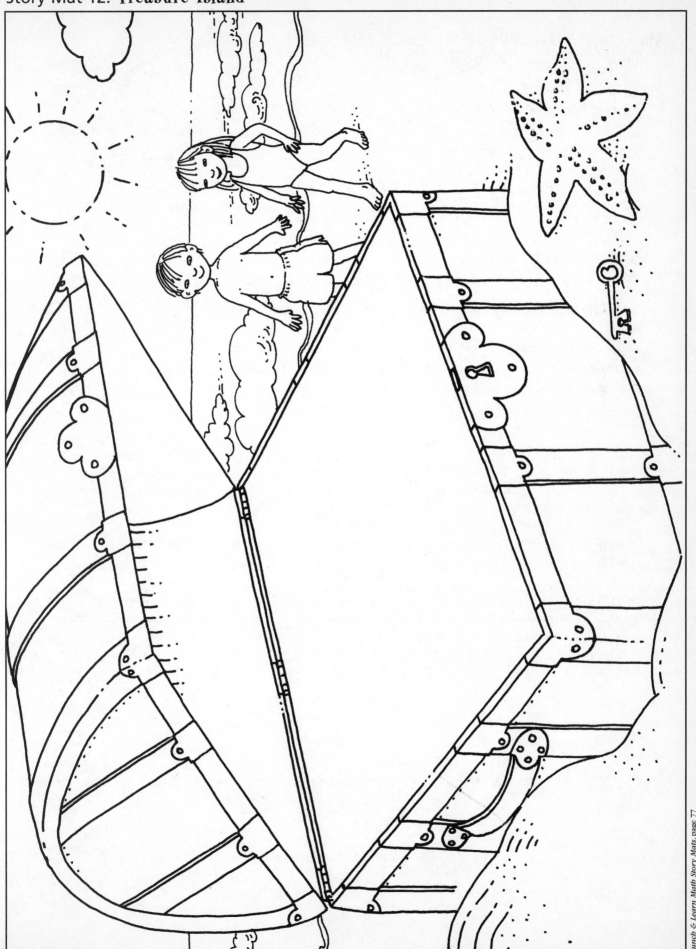

Tooth Tales

Read-Aloud Story 1:
Darlene's Trip to the Dentist

Darlene was going to the dentist for a checkup. She sat down in the big chair. "Open wide," said the dentist, "let's count your teeth!"

"How many teeth do you think you have?" he asked Darlene. Darlene made a guess and the dentist began to count. First he counted the top teeth. 1, 2, 3, 4, 5, 6, 7, 8, 9, 10! Next he counted the bottom row of teeth.

Darlene had the same number of teeth on the bottom as she did on the top. How many teeth does Darlene have all together?

"Good job, Darlene," said the dentist, "and I counted zero cavities!"

Read-Aloud Story 2: Tammy's Loose Tooth

Tammy has ten teeth, and four are loose! One falls out in September. The tooth fairy puts one dime and three nickels in Tammy's piggy bank. In October one more tooth falls out. The tooth fairy puts two dimes and a nickel in her bank. Tammy's last two teeth fall out in November. The tooth fairy puts two quarters in her bank. Tammy counts up the coins. How much money does she have?

Darlene's Trip to the Dentist

Materials

✳ copies of Story Mat 13 (page 83)

✳ miniature marshmallows, 10 per child (or copies of manipulatives, page 84)

Target Skills

⚙ counting
⚙ estimation
⚙ matching, one-to-one correspondence
⚙ basic number operations (addition, subtraction)

1 Distribute the mats. Instruct children to just listen and look while you read through the story one time.

2 Distribute the marshmallows or paper manipulatives and read through the story a second time, pausing after each sentence. Have children use the marshmallows or paper manipulatives to represent the teeth in the story. Check for understanding after each sentence.

Math Talk

✳ What addition strategies did you use to come up with the answer to the dentist's question?

✳ How close was your estimate of the number of Darlene's teeth? Was it more? Less? How do you know?

Journal Extension

Ask children to draw a picture illustrating Darlene's mouth. Have them draw ten teeth on the bottom and a different number on top. Students can write a number sentence to match their drawing.

Here's More

Explain to students that at their age they have teeth called primary teeth—20 to be exact! Tell students that when they are adults they will have permanent teeth. Explain that they will have 16 teeth on the bottom. Ask students how many they will have if the amount on top is the same.

Assessment TIPS

◆ Collect student's math journals and check their illustrations and number sentences to see if they match. Also check student's sums to gauge how proficient they are in adding with ten.

Read-Aloud Story 2

Tammy's Loose Tooth

Materials

✴ copies of Story Mat 13 (page 83)

✴ miniature marshmallows, 10 per child (or copies of manipulatives, page 84)

✴ coins (or copies of coin manipulatives, page 54; 4 quarters, 10 dimes, and 20 nickels per child)

Target Skills

◎ counting
◎ money
◎ basic number facts (addition)

1 Distribute the mats. Instruct children to just listen and look while you read through the story one time.

2 Distribute the marshmallows or paper manipulatives and read through the story a second time, pausing after each sentence. Have children use the marshmallows or paper manipulatives to represent the teeth in the story, and the money to work out the problems posed. Check for understanding after each sentence.

Math Talk

✳ Did Tammy get the same amount of money for each tooth?

✳ How much money did she get for each tooth?

✳ Explain your strategy for counting up the amount of money Tammy has in her bank.

Journal Extension

Have children illustrate several ways to make one dollar. Challenge them to discover how many nickels equal one dollar, how many dimes equal one dollar, and how many quarters equal one dollar.

Assessment TIPS

◆ Have children focus on the concept of 25 cents. Ask children to use their manipulatives to help them draw all the different ways to make 25 cents using quarters, dimes, nickels, and pennies.

Here's More

Help children pair off. Have the first student be the tooth fairy and the second student be Tammy. They can play a simple counting game to practice counting different amounts of money. Here's how:

✳ Have both children share a story mat. The first student should have a variety of coins that equal one dollar. The second student should place ten teeth in Tammy's mouth on the story mat.

✳ The second student should remove any number of teeth from Tammy's mouth that he or she chooses.

✳ Instead of paying 25 cents for each tooth that is lost, the tooth fairy should place one coin in the piggy bank for each tooth that fell out. Each coin can be of any amount the first student chooses.

✳ Have children continue this activity, removing a small amount of teeth for each turn and putting coins in the piggy bank, until all of Tammy's teeth have fallen out.

✳ They should then count the amount of money inside the piggy bank to practice their counting skills with money. They can also count how much money the tooth fairy has left.

✳ The players can switch roles and play the game again. Each time the game is played again, the tooth fairy can select a different combination of coins that add up to one dollar.

Munch & Learn Math Story Mats, page 83
Scholastic Professional Books

Story Mat 13: **Tooth Tales: Manipulatives**

The Three Little Pigs

Read-Aloud Story 1: Building a House of Sticks

The big, bad wolf had ten sticks piled in his wheelbarrow. "Please, sir," said the little pig. "May I buy some sticks to build my house?"

"Gr-r-reat," the wolf growled.

The little pig bought enough sticks to build his house one-quarter of the way up. How many did he need to do this? Then the little pig bought enough sticks to build his house one-half of the way up. How many had he bought all together?

"It's time for my lunch break," growled the big, bad wolf. "I have to go huffing and puffing. You can buy the rest of your sticks tomorrow." How many sticks did the wolf have left in his wheelbarrow? How many sticks did the pig need to buy the next day to finish his house?

Read-Aloud Story 2: Huffing and Puffing

The little pig built his house three-quarters of the way up. Use your markers to show what he did. Guess how many more sticks he needs to finish building his house. Count out that number of sticks. Now help him build his house.

Along came the big, bad wolf. "Little pig! Little pig! Let me in!"

"Not by the hair on my chinny chin chin!" the pig said.

"Then I'll huff and I'll puff and I'll blow your house down!" growled the wolf. First he huffed and puffed away sticks so the house was only one-half of the way up. The wolf put the sticks in his wheelbarrow. How many did he get? Second, the wolf huffed and puffed so the house was only one quarter of the way up. How many sticks did he get? Third, the wolf huffed and puffed the house away. He put all the sticks in his wheelbarrow.

The little pig ran to the house of bricks. "You can't catch me," the little pig squealed. "You'll just have to eat sticks instead!" How many sticks did the wolf eat?

Building a House of Sticks

Materials

✳ copies of Story Mat 14 (page 89)

✳ thin, small pretzel sticks, about 20 per child (or copies of manipulatives, page 90)

1 Distribute the mats. Instruct children to just listen and look while you read through the story one time.

2 Distribute the pretzels or paper manipulatives and read through the story a second time, pausing after each sentence. Have children use the pretzels or paper manipulatives (arranged horizontally) to represent the sticks in the story. Check for understanding after each sentence. Instruct children not to place the sticks above the mark represented for each fraction. You might have them draw a line across the house to mark $\frac{1}{4}$ and $\frac{1}{2}$ of the way up.

Math Talk

✳ How did you know how many sticks the pig needed the next day? (Answers will vary depending on the kind of manipulatives students use.)

✳ How did you know where to stop building at each step?

Journal Extension

Have children write number sentences that represent the sticks the pig added to the house and the sticks the wolf took away from his wheelbarrow.

Target Skills

⚙ fractions
⚙ nonstandard measurement (volume)
⚙ counting
⚙ basic number operations (addition, subtraction, multiplication)

Here's More

Make a kit for children to use as they explore the concept of fractions. Use pink construction paper to make three pigs and green construction paper to make a rectangular house. Then cut two green construction paper halves that stack together over the house. Use a permanent marker to label each piece $\frac{1}{2}$. Use blue construction paper to make another rectangular house. Cut three blue construction paper thirds that stack together over the house. Label each piece $\frac{1}{3}$. Use purple construction paper to make a third rectangular house. Cut four purple pieces of construction paper that stack together over the house. Label each piece $\frac{1}{4}$. Place all the pieces in a plastic bag with a zipper closing. Let children take the bag to their seats and build the fraction houses for the three pigs, placing the pieces over the matching color of houses.

Assessment TIPS

* As children help the pig build his house of sticks, walk around the room and check to see that each student adds the correct amount of sticks for each fraction.

Read-Aloud Story 2

Huffing and Puffing

Materials

* copies of Story Mat 14 (page 89)

* pretzel sticks, about 20 per child (or copies of manipulatives, page 90)

1 Distribute the mats. Instruct children to just listen and look while you read through the story one time.

2 Distribute the pretzels or paper manipulatives and read through the story a second time, pausing after each sentence. Have children use the pretzels or paper manipulatives to represent the sticks in the story. Check for understanding after each sentence.

Target Skills

* fractions
* estimation
* counting
* basic number facts (addition, subtraction)
* order
* nonstandard measurement (volume)

Math Talk

✳ Did you guess the right number of sticks the pig needed to build his house? Did you guess too many? Too few? Or just the right amount? How did you guess?

Journal Extension

Have children draw three houses for the little pigs. Then have them divide the houses into halves, thirds, and fourths, with labels for each.

Here's More

Give children large blocks to practice addition and subtraction skills as they build houses for the three little pigs! Collect empty cereal boxes and place them in a laundry basket (or cover the boxes with brown paper to resemble bricks).

Write word problems on large index cards such as the following:

✳ The pig built a house with 8 bricks stacked on top of each other. The wolf blew away 4 bricks. How many bricks were left at the pig's house?

✳ The wolf gave the pig 3 bricks. Then the wolf gave the pig 6 bricks. Then the pig built the house. How many bricks did the pig use to build the house?

✳ The wolf had 10 bricks. He sold 3 bricks to the pig. How many bricks did the wolf have left?

✳ Let children use the laundry basket of bricks to stack them and work out the answers to the word problems.

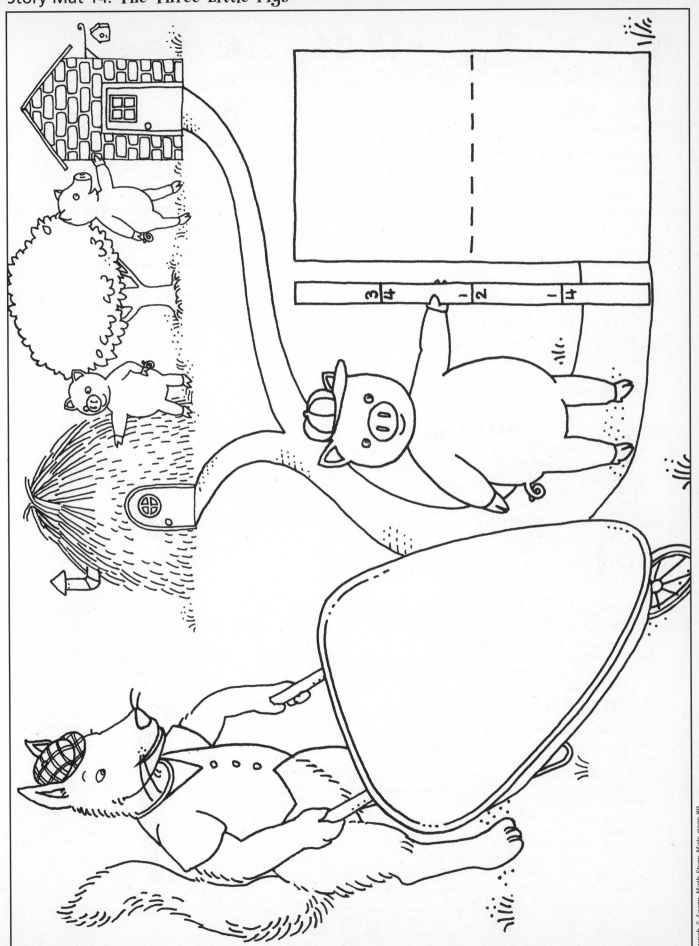

Story Mat 14: The Three Little Pigs: Manipulatives

Dinosaur Dan

Read-Aloud Story 1: Painting Patterns

Dinosaur Dan likes to paint patterns. Help him by closing your eyes, reaching into the container of markers and picking three markers. Put these in the boxes next to the number 1. Look at the pattern he made! Dinosaur Dan wants to make that pattern all across the first row. Use your markers to show his pattern.

Now Dinosaur Dan reaches into the container and picks out two more markers. He places these in the boxes next to the number 2. Look at the pattern he made! He makes that pattern all across the second row. Show it with your markers.

Dinosaur Dan makes patterns across the third, fourth, and fifth rows. Use your markers to help him make up these patterns. What a nice picture!

Read-Aloud Story 2: Picture Surprises

Dinosaur Dan likes to paint pictures on a graph—and you can help him. He needs you to place a different marker in the box next to each number. Then, to complete the picture, reach into your container of markers—no peeking!—take out a marker, and place it in the box next to the marker it matches. If you keep choosing markers without peeking, which row do you think will fill up first? Try it and find out.

Painting Patterns

Materials

✳ copies of Story Mat 15 (page 95)

✳ bowls of about 50 snack items each with an assortment of 5 shapes such as cereal with marshmallow shapes, mixed nuts, gummy snacks, or crackers (or copies of manipulatives, page 96)

1 Distribute mats. Instruct children to just listen while you read through the story one time.

2 Distribute the edible or paper manipulatives. Read through the story a second time. Have children use the edible or paper manipulatives to create the patterns on the graph. By the time children are making a pattern along the top row of the graph, they may not have enough markers with a particular attribute left to complete their pattern. Encourage them to share and exchange markers with other children to complete their patterns.

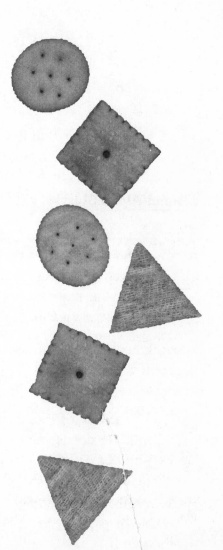

Math Talk

✳ What does the word *pattern* mean to you?

✳ What would happen if the graph were longer? What would happen next in each pattern?

✳ How did you know how to continue your pattern?

Journal Extension

Have children draw or write about a pattern they see in the classroom. Encourage them to use shape, number, and color words.

Make a class pattern book. Have each child illustrate a pattern they see in their house. When they bring their pictures back to class, have them share the pictures with the class and then bind them together in a book. Children can look through the pattern book during free time.

Assessment TIPS

◆ Do children understand the concept of patterns? Can they create their own patterns? Read through the story another time, having children build different patterns on the graph as you observe their work.

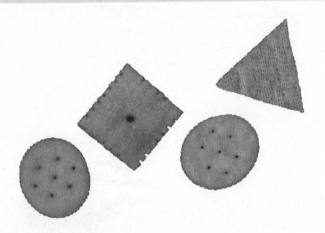

Read-Aloud Story 2

Picture Surprises

Materials

✳ copies of Story Mat 15 (page 95)

✳ snack item that has an assortment of 5 shapes such as cereal with marshmallow shapes, mixed nuts, gummy snacks, or cracker shapes; 1 bowl of about 50 items per child (or copies of manipulatives, page 96)

Target Skills

⊙ graphing
⊙ probability
⊙ counting
⊙ position
⊙ matching

1 Distribute the mats. Instruct children to just listen while you read through the story one time.

2 Read through the story a second time. Distribute the edible or paper manipulatives to play the game on the graph.

Math Talk

⁂ Share your results. Can you explain why some of the results were the same and some were different?

⁂ What does the word *chance* mean to you? Do you know a larger word that means the same thing?

⁂ Share the word *probability* with children. Does it sound like another word (*probably, probable*)?

⁂ Can you predict what will happen if you play the game again?

⁂ Did everyone reach the end of his or her row at the same time? Why or why not?

⁂ Which marker "won" most often?

Journal Extension

Have children dictate or write about whether the results of the game were as they expected. Or, have them describe their favorite game and how it is played. Does it use a number cube? Is it a game that depends on probability?

Here's More

Divide the class into five teams. Draw a large graph similar to Dinosaur Dan's on the board. Have a large bowl of snacks or markers that have five different shapes in it. Assign each team a different marker to use in its row on the graph by drawing a picture of each item in the first blank box of the group's row. Take turns having a member from each team come forward and choose a marker from the bowl without looking. Draw that item in the corresponding row. Whichever team's row is completed first wins the game. Play the game several times, keeping a tally of the winning teams.

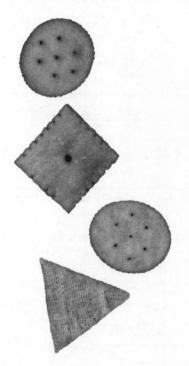

94

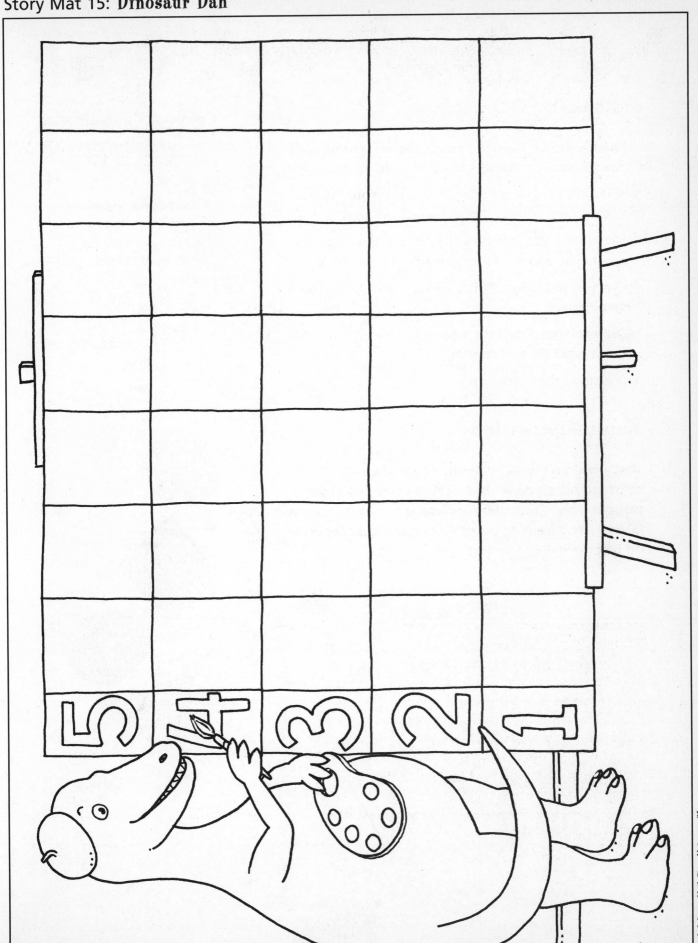

Story Mat 15: Dinosaur Dan: Manipulatives

Story Mat 15: Dinosaur Dan: Manipulatives